10th Anniversary Limited Edition

Timeless Patterns
for Today's Quilter

by Kent Ward

The Best of *Traditional Quiltworks* and *Quilting Today* magazines

CHITRA PUBLICATIONS
Your best value in quilting!

First printing: 1997

Library of Congress Cataloging-in-Publication Data

Timeless patterns for today's quilter : the best of Traditional
    quiltworks and Quilting today magazines / [compiled and edited by
    Kent Ward]. — 10th anniversary limited ed.
        p.   cm.
    ISBN 1-885588-14-3
    1. Patchwork — Patterns. 2. Quilting —Patterns. 3. Patchwork
quilts.   I. Ward, Kent.   II. Traditional quiltworks.   III. Quilting
today.
TT835.T49 1997
746.46'041—dc21   96-49567
                                                          CIP

Compiled and Edited by Kent Ward
Design and Illustration: Kimberly L. Grace
Cover photography: Guy Cali Associates, Inc., Clarks Summit, PA
Inside photography: Stephen J. Appel Photography, Vestal, NY; Ken Jacques Photography, San Diego, CA, and Van Zandbergen Photography, Brackney, PA

The hoop on the front cover was graciously supplied by:
Jasmine Heirlooms
500 Fairview Drive • Greenville, SC • 29609
Phone: (864) 292-0735

Have you ever stopped to .think that the beautiful antique quilts we admire were once contemporary quilts? The same goes for the quilts we create today. Even if we make a traditional style quilt and sew every stitch by hand, it's still a contemporary quilt. Why? Because it was produced by a quilter in our own time.

The quilts I selected for this book are contemporary in that sense. Each was made by an American quilter during the last decade. On the other hand, each has very strong traditional roots—each quilter used a favorite time-honored pattern like Schoolhouse, Grandmother's Fan or Log Cabin.

What, then, distinguishes these quilts from their antique predecessors? It's that personal touch that every quilter added. For one quilter, it's an unusual color scheme, like the stark black and white of Lynda Carswell's "Expanding Universe." For Pauline Warren, it was arranging scrappy Delectable Mountains blocks to form an eight-pointed star. Even when a quilter uses antique fabric, as Norma Grasse did in "An Old Schoolhouse," the resulting quilt is still a product of our own time. Although her quilt has an old-fashioned feeling, the pink stars formed by the pieced sashing add an explosive energy that says "now."

But these quiltmakers don't have to be the only ones having fun. You can give a personal touch to every quilt you make. As you prepare to use one of the patterns in this book, ask yourself the simple question popularized by our friend Sharyn Craig— "What if...?" What if you make the quilt using plaids? What if you substitute dark green for the light background fabric? What if you try a pieced border instead of a plain one? Remember—it's your quilt. Enjoy it.

Kent

Contents

Patterns

🥛 Beginner 🥛🥛 Intermediate 🥛🥛🥛 Advanced

Jacob's Ladder

Break the rules—we'll show you how!

QUILT SIZE: 63" x 81"
BLOCK SIZE: 9" square

MATERIALS
Yardage is estimated for 44" fabric.
For each of 31 Jacob's Ladder blocks:
- 7" x 9" piece of light
- 7" x 9" piece of medium
- 7" x 9" piece of dark

NOTE: *Your total for all 31 blocks will be approximately 1 5/8 yards each of lights, mediums and darks.*

Also:
- 1 1/4 yards green
- 1 1/4 yards gold
- 1 yard off-white
- 4 yards of fabric for the backing and binding
- 67" x 85" piece of batting

CUTTING
All dimensions include a 1/4" seam allowance. Use the templates provided or cut without templates.
- Cut 16: 9 7/8" squares, green, then cut each in half diagonally
- Cut 16: 9 7/8" squares, gold, then cut each in half diagonally
- Cut 124: A, off-white; or cut sixty-two 3 7/8" squares in half diagonally

For each of 31 Jacob's Ladder blocks:
- Cut 4: A, medium; or cut two 3 7/8" squares in half diagonally
- Cut 10: B, dark; or cut ten 2" squares
- Cut 10: B, light; or cut ten 2" squares

PIECING
- Stitch a large gold triangle to a large green triangle, as shown, forming a large pieced square. Trim the "dog ears" that form at the corners and press the seam toward the darker fabric. Make 32.

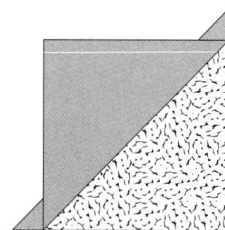

- Stitch an off-white A to a medium A, forming a pieced square. Trim and press. Make 4 per block, or 124 pieced squares in 31 sets of 4.
- Stack the 10 light B squares and 10 dark B squares in separate piles. Chain stitch them together in pairs.

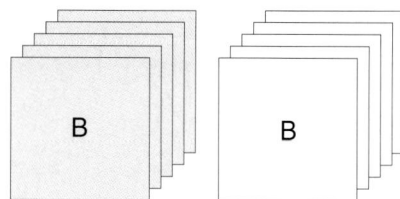

- Join the pairs to form Four Patches. Make 5.

- Lay out 5 Four Patches and 4 pieced squares to form a Jacob's Ladder block. Stitch the squares into rows, then join the rows to complete the block. Press. Be aware that the dark squares follow one diagonal and the light squares the opposite diagonal. If you look closely at the photo you can see where quiltmaker Kathy

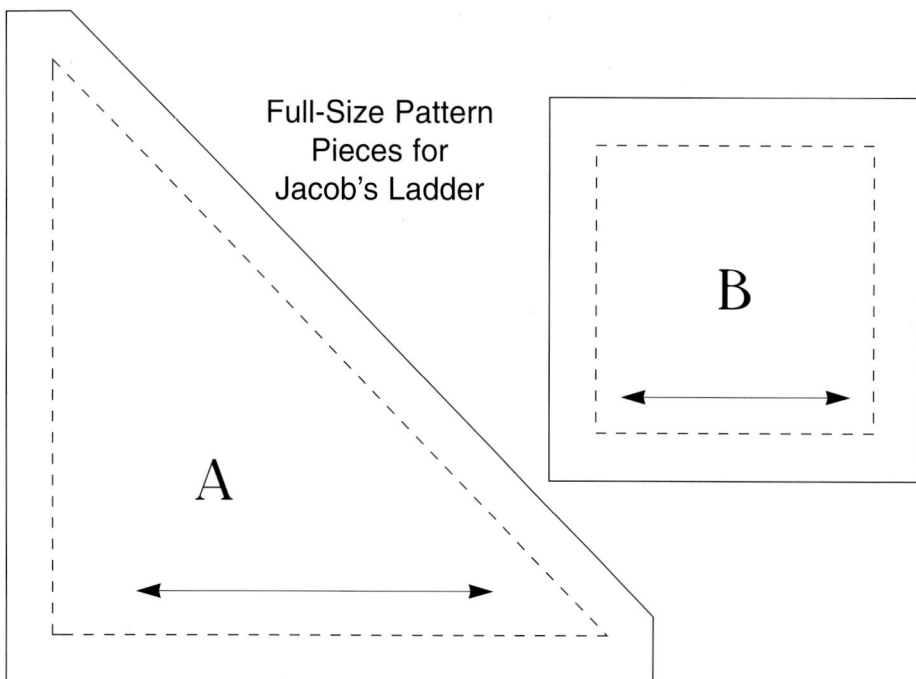

Full-Size Pattern
Pieces for
Jacob's Ladder

A

B

After taking a color study course from Jo Anne Parisi at "Calico Stitchery" in West Springfield, Massachusetts, Kathleen Kalinowski, now of Cary, North Carolina, created this handsome **Jacob's Ladder quilt** (63" x 81"). The challenge was to make "antique" quilts from new fabric. Kathy planned an assortment of delightful "mistakes" for her quilt. How many can you find? Our pattern tells you how to create your own new-antique quilt—mistakes included!

Kalinowski broke this "rule" to imitate the appearance of an old quilt. Have fun and plan a mistake or two! Make 31 blocks.

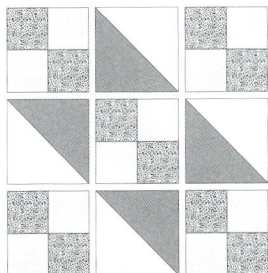

ASSEMBLY

• Referring to the quilt photo as needed, lay out the blocks and large green and gold pieced squares in 9 horizontal rows of 7. Rearrange the Jacob's Ladder blocks to suit your color preference.

NOTE: *The rule for this layout is that the dark squares in each block follow the same diagonal as the one created by the large green and gold pieced squares. Feel free to break this rule.*

• Finish the quilt as described in the *General Directions*. The diagram to the right shows Kathy's quilting design. Use the 2 1/2" x 44" strips for the binding.

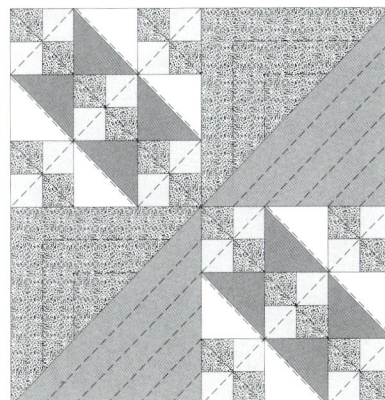

Aim for the Stars

Stars and Attic Windows team up for a winning combination!

"Aim for the Stars" (58 1/2" x 85 1/2") by nationally known quiltmaker and teacher Sharyn Craig. Sharyn's inspiration for this quilt was a traditional pattern called Sun Ray's Quilt. Attic Windows sashing adds an intriguing three-dimensional quality, while a healthy variety of fabrics gives it plenty of eye appeal. Sharyn made this quilt as a high school graduation gift for her daughter, Amy.

QUILT SIZE: 58 1/2" x 85 1/2"
BLOCK SIZE: 7 1/2"

MATERIALS
Yardage is estimated for 44" fabric.
- Assorted medium and dark scraps totaling at least 1 3/4 yards, for the stars; or a 5 1/2" x 11" piece for each star
- 2 1/2 yards, cream, for the background
- Assorted rose-colored prints totaling at least 3/4 yard, for the sashing; you'll need 1/8 yard of at least one
- Assorted turquoise prints totaling at least 3/4 yard, for the sashing; you'll need 1/8 yard of at least one
- 2 1/2 yards, large print, for the border
- 5/8 yard fabric for the binding
- 5 yards fabric for the backing
- 63" x 90" piece of batting

CUTTING
Pattern pieces are full size and include a 1/4" seam allowance, as do all dimensions given. We recommend making a sample block before cutting fabric for the whole quilt. Cut the lengthwise border strips parallel to the selvage.

For each of 40 star blocks:
- Cut 1: A, medium or dark scrap; or cut 3" squares
- Cut 4: B and BR, same scrap fabric as A

In addition:
- Cut 160: A, cream; or cut twelve 3" x 44" strips and cut 3" squares from them
- Cut 160: C, cream
- Cut 2: 2" x 44" strips, turquoise—cut these from the 1/8 yard
- Cut 40: D, turquoise
- Cut 2: 2" x 44" strips, rose—cut these from the 1/8 yard
- Cut 40: DR, rose
- Cut 2: 6 1/2" x 63" lengthwise strips, large print
- Cut 2: 6 1/2" x 90" lengthwise strips, large print
- Cut 8: 2 1/2" x 44" strips, fabric for the binding

PIECING
- Take the medium or dark pieces for a single block—one A, 4 B's and 4 BR's, all cut from the same fabric. You'll also need 4 cream A's and 4 cream C's.
- Stitch a B and BR to the 2 longer sides of each C, making the "star points."

- Lay out the star points with the A squares in 3 rows, as shown. Stitch them into rows, then join the rows to complete the block. Make 40 blocks.

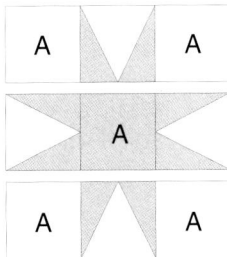

- To add the Attic Windows sashing, sew a turquoise D to the bottom edge of each block, as shown. Start and stop stitching 1/4" from the edge of the fabric. In the same way, sew a rose DR to the left side of each block.

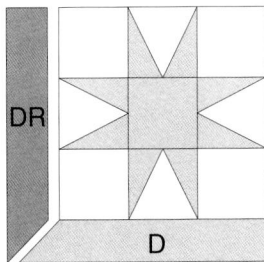

- To sew the short diagonal seam between the D and DR, fold the block in half diagonally, right sides together. Line up the diagonal edges of the D and DR, then stitch the seam from the inside toward the outside edge.

ASSEMBLY
- Lay out the blocks on the floor or your design wall, in 8 horizontal rows of 5. Reposition individual blocks until you find the most pleasing arrangement. Be sure to turn each block so that the rose strip is on the left and the turquoise strip is on the bottom.
- Stitch the blocks into 8 rows, then join the rows, matching seams.
- Join the two 2" x 44" rose strips end to end. Center and stitch them to the quilt's right side, then trim off the excess.
- Join the two 2" x 44" turquoise strips end to end. Center and sew this strip to the top of quilt; trim off the excess.
- Center and stitch the 6 1/2" x 90" large print border strips to the left and right sides of the quilt. Start and stop stitching 1/4" from the edge of the fabric. In the same way, center and stitch the 6 1/2" x 63" large print border strips to the top and bottom edges. Miter the corners, referring to the *General Directions* as needed.
- Finish the quilt as described in the *General Directions*, using the 2 1/2" x 44" strips for the binding.

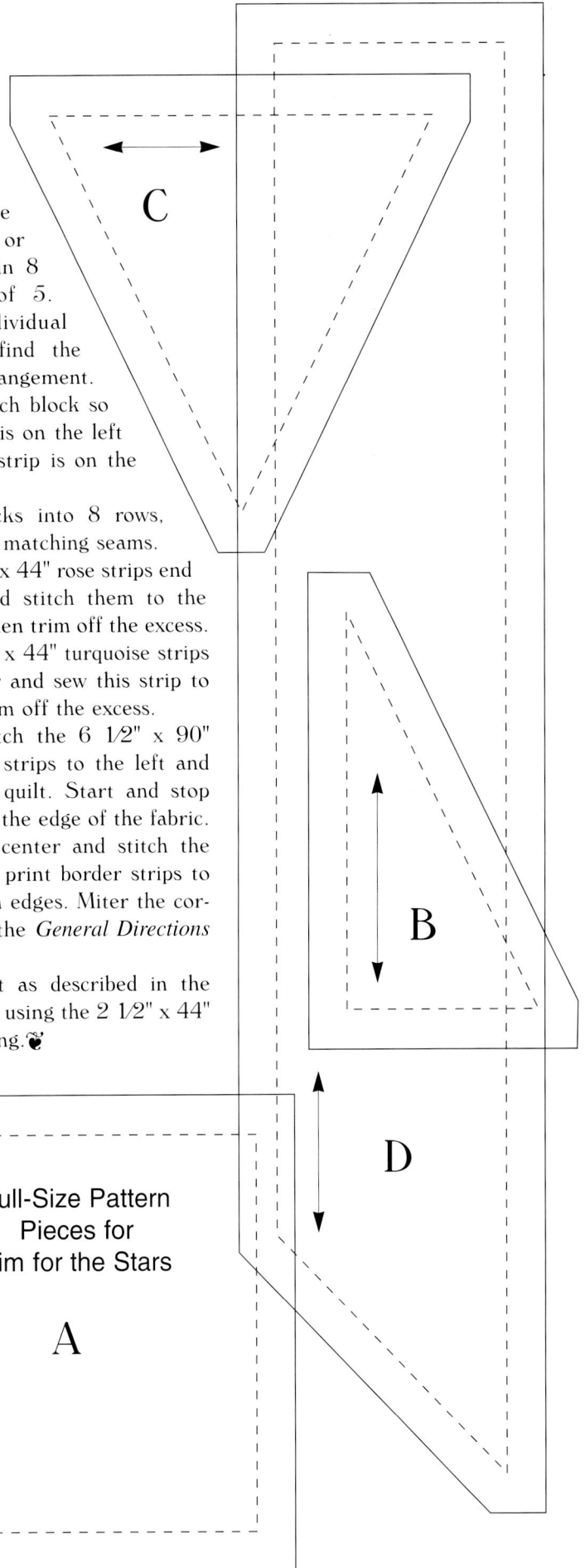

Full-Size Pattern Pieces for Aim for the Stars

C

B

D

A

An Old Schoolhouse

Houses and stars in a winning combination!

QUILT SIZE: 75" square
BLOCK SIZE: 9" square

MATERIALS

Yardage is estimated for 44" fabric.
• Scraps of red print, or 1/4 yard, for the chimneys and doors
• Scraps of light print, or 1/4 yard, for the windows
• Scraps of black print at least 9" square for the 25 houses—you can get 4 houses from a quilter's quarter (18" x 22")
• Scraps of dark prints at least 6 1/4" square, totaling 1 1/4 yards, for the 44 appliquéd stars
• 3/4 yard pink print, for the sashing intersections—2 different prints were used in the sample quilt
• 2 yards black solid, for the pieced borders and binding
• 3 1/2 yards white print, for the background
• 4 1/2 yards backing fabric
• 79" square of batting

CUTTING

Pattern pieces are full size; all except the star appliqué pattern include a 1/4" seam allowance, as do all dimensions given. After cutting, you may wish to stack like pieces together and label the stack with the size or letter designation.

For each of the 25 blocks:
• Cut 2: 1 1/2" squares, red, for the chimneys
• Cut 1: 1 1/2" x 3 1/2" strip, red, for the door
• Cut 1: 1 1/2" square, window fabric
• Cut 2: 1 1/2" x 2 1/2" rectangles, window fabric
• Cut 1: A and AR, house fabric
• Cut 1: B, house fabric

• Cut 1: C, house fabric
• Cut 1: D, house fabric
• Cut 1: 1 1/2" x 4 1/2" strip, house fabric
• Cut 2: 2" x 3 1/2" rectangles, house fabric
• Cut 2: 1 1/2" x 5" strips, house fabric
• Cut 2: 1 1/4" x 2 1/2" strips, house fabric
• Cut 1: 1 1/2" x 2 1/2" rectangle, house fabric

In addition:
• Cut 25: 1 1/2" x 3 1/2" strips, white
• Cut 25: 1 1/2" x 5 1/2" strips, white
• Cut 50: 2 1/2" squares, white
• Cut 25: E, white
• Cut 25: F, white
• Cut 25: G and GR, white
• Cut 25: 1" x 4 1/2" strips, white
• Cut 60: H, white
• Cut 120: J and JR, pink
• Cut 36: 2 1/2" squares, pink
• Cut 5: 15" squares, white
• Cut 5: 15" squares, black solid
• Cut 44: Stars (appliqué pieces), assorted prints

NOTE: *There is some variation among the border stars of the sample quilt. To maintain the folk art flavor, use the star pattern "loosely," and/or give your scissors free rein when cutting the stars.*
• Cut 7: 6 1/2" x 44" strips, white
• Cut 7: 2 1/2" x 44" strips, black solid, for the binding

PIECING

• Take the black print pieces you cut for a single block. Sew an A and AR to opposite sides of a 1 1/2" square of window fabric. Sew a B triangle to the top of this unit and C strip to the bottom.

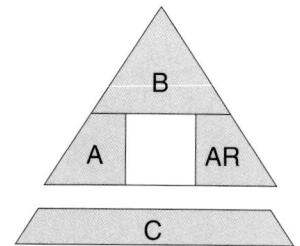

• Sew an E strip to the left of the D. Then sew an F strip to the bottom of this unit.

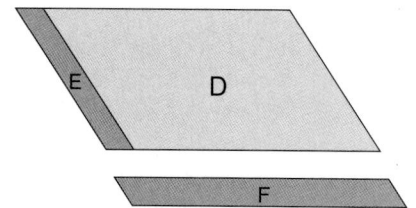

• Join the pieced units. Sew a G to the left end and a GR to the right, completing the roof section.

• Sew 1 1/2" red squares to both ends of a 1 1/2" x 3 1/2" white strip. Sew a 1 1/2" x 5 1/2" white strip to the top of the unit. Join 2 1/2" white squares to both ends, completing the sky section.

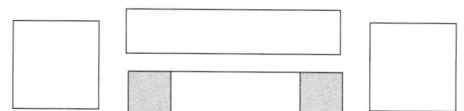

• Sew 2" x 3 1/2" black rectangles to both long sides of a 1 1/2" x 3 1/2" red strip. Stitch a 1 1/2" x 4 1/2" black strip to the top of the unit, then a 1" x

"An Old Schoolhouse" (75" x 75") by Norma Grasse of Perkasie, Pennsylvania, combines the best of old and new. While the block pattern is a time-honored favorite and the dark fabrics are antique, Norma purchased a new white print for the background and machine stitched the blocks. Appliquéd stars enliven the border.

4 1/2" white strip to the right side of the unit. This is the door section.

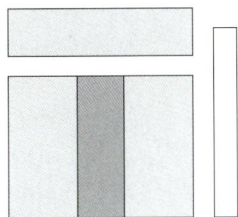

• Sew a 1 1/2" x 2 1/2" black rectangle between two 1 1/2" x 2 1/2" rectangles of window fabric. Stitch 1 1/4" x 2 1/2" black strips to the left and right ends of the unit. Then sew 1 1/2" x 5" black strips to the top and bottom of the unit. This is the window section.

• Stitch the door section to the left of the window section.
• Join the 3 pieced units to complete the Schoolhouse block. Make 25 blocks.

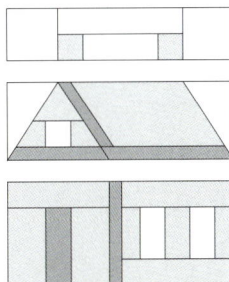

• To make the pieced sashing strips, sew a J and JR to one end of an H. Do the same with the other end of the H. Make 60 pieced sashing strips.

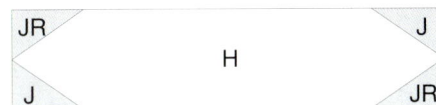

QUICK PIECING

• For quick-pieced half-square triangles, lay the 15" white squares wrong side up. Starting 1/2" down from the top edge and 1/2" in from the left, mark a grid of 2 3/8" squares on the fabric. Use a pencil and a wide ruler. Make the grid 6 squares by 6 squares—for a total of 36 squares.
• Draw a diagonal line through each

9

Full-Size Pattern
Pieces for
An Old Schoolhouse.
Pattern begins
on page 8.

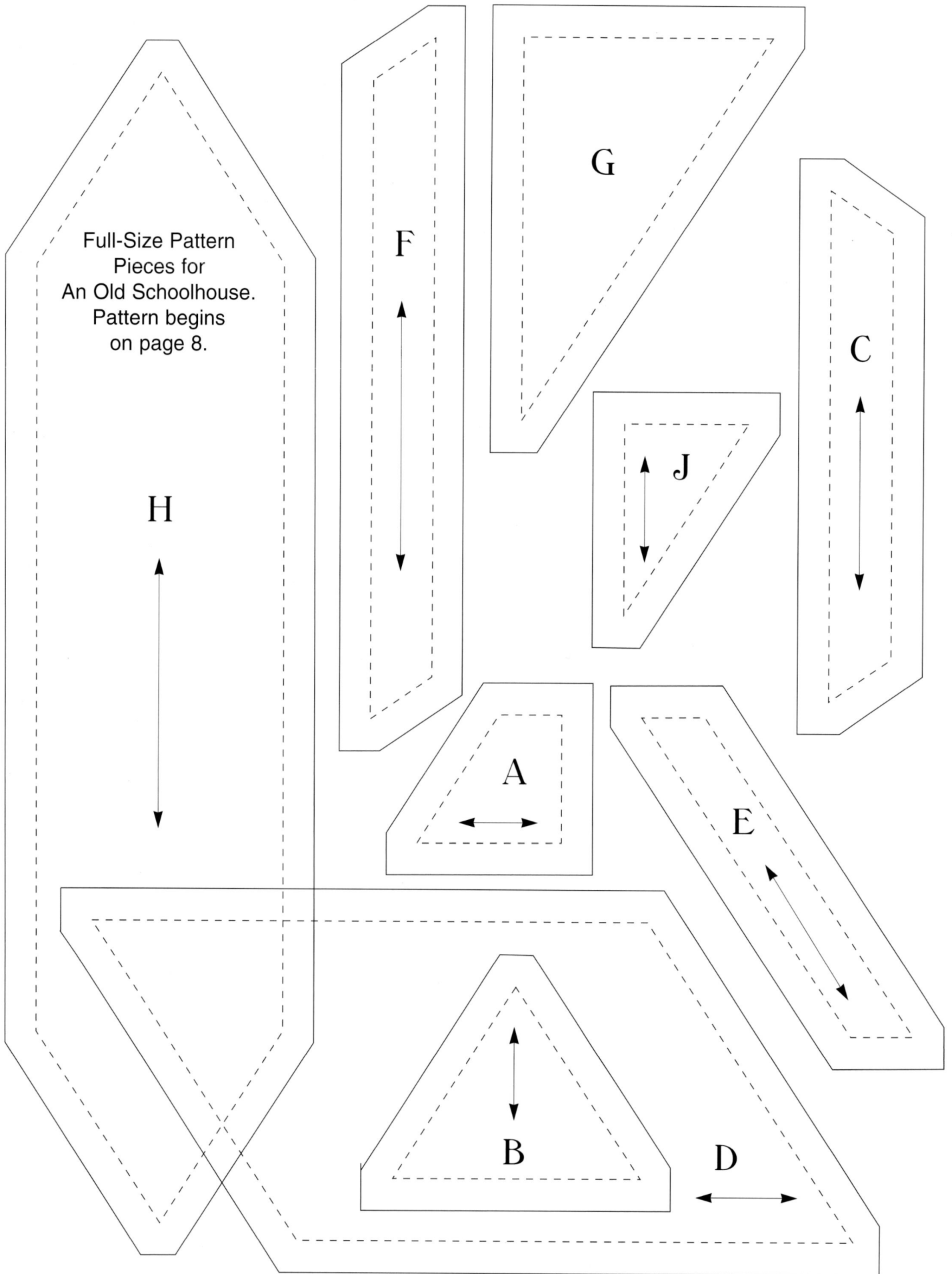

F

G

C

H

J

A

E

B

D

of the grid squares.

• Lay a marked white square and a 15" black solid square right sides together. Smooth out all wrinkles and pin.

• With the sewing machine's stitch length set at 12 to 15 stitches per inch, sew exactly 1/4" both to the left and the right side of each marked diagonal line.

NOTE: *If you prefer, mark the sewing lines on both sides of each diagonal line before pinning the 2 layers of fabric together.*

• After stitching, cut on all the vertical and horizontal lines, making 36 squares. Then cut each square in half on the marked diagonal line.

• Open up the resulting triangles and press. You may have to pick a few stitches from the points of each triangle. Yield: 72 black and white pieced squares.

• Repeat the process with the 4 remaining 15" white squares.

ASSEMBLY

• Lay out your 25 Schoolhouse blocks in 5 rows of 5. If necessary, rearrange the blocks until you are happy with the arrangement.

• Working with one horizontal row at a time, stitch pieced sashing strips between the blocks in each row. Also stitch pieced sashing strips at both ends of the row. The finished row should have 5 blocks and 6 pieced sashing strips. Press, then return the completed row to your layout. Do this for all 5 rows.

• Make 6 sashing rows, each consisting of 5 pieced sashing strips and six 2 1/2" pink squares. Sew the sashing strips and squares together alternately.

• Lay the sashing rows between the rows of blocks. Lay the last 2 sashing rows at the top and bottom edges of the layout. Join the rows, matching the seams.

ASSEMBLY

• Make a row of 38 black and white pieced squares. Orient them as indicated. Make 3 more identical rows of 38.

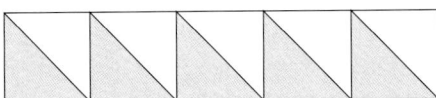

• Sew a row of pieced squares to the top edge of the quilt. Position it so that the white triangles will be at the outer edge. Sew another row of pieced squares to the bottom edge of the quilt, white triangles to the outside.

• Referring to the photo as needed, lay the other 2 rows of pieced squares along the left and right sides of the quilt. White triangles to the outside. Place a single pieced square in each corner and decide how you wish to position it.

• Sew the pieced squares to the ends of the rows, then join the rows to the quilt.

• Take three 6 1/2" x 44" white strips. Cut one in half and sew a half to one end of each of the other strips. Trim the strips to 60 1/2", or the width of your quilt top.

• Arrange 10 stars more or less evenly along each 60 1/2" border strip. Don't position them all identically—refer to the photo. Baste them down, then appliqué them in place.

• Sew the appliquéd borders to 2 opposite sides of the quilt.

• Sew the remaining 6 1/2" x 44" white

strips in pairs, end to end. Trim them to 72 1/2", or the length of your quilt top. Arrange 12 stars along each. Baste, then appliqué them.

• Sew the appliquéd borders to the long sides of your quilt.

• Make a row of 48 black and white pieced squares. Position them as indicated. Make 3 more identical rows of 48.

• Sew a row of pieced squares to the top edge of the quilt. Place it so that the black triangles will be at the outer edge. In the same way, sew a row of pieced squares to the bottom edge of the quilt.

• Lay the other 2 rows of pieced squares along the left and right sides of the quilt, black triangles to the outside. Place a single pieced square in each corner.

• Sew the pieced squares to the ends of the rows, then join the rows to the quilt.

• Finish the quilt as described in the *General Directions*, using the 2 1/2" x 44" strips for the binding. ❦

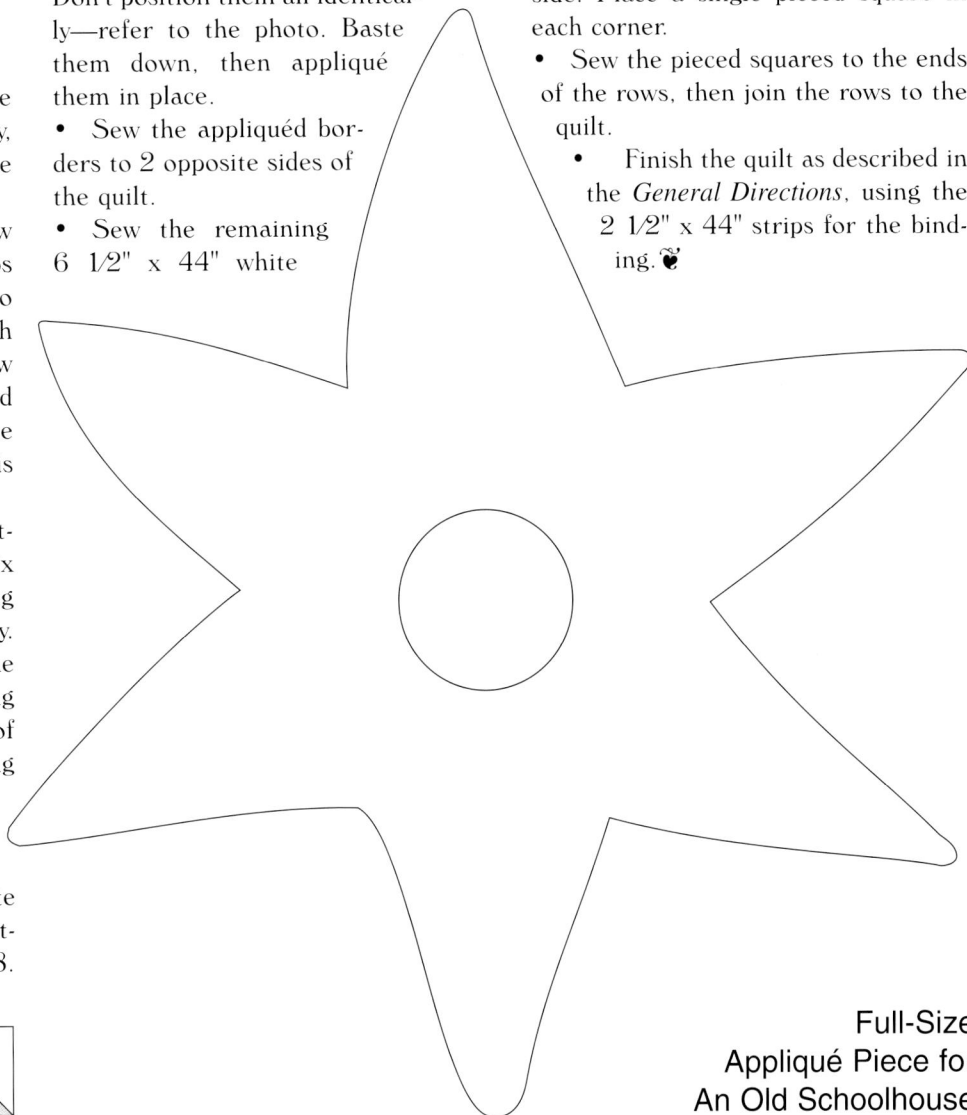

Full-Size
Appliqué Piece for
An Old Schoolhouse

Drunkard's Path

Make this eye-catching quilt from your choicest scraps!

QUILT SIZE: 54" x 66"
BLOCK SIZE: 12" square

MATERIALS

Yardage is estimated for 44" fabric.
• Assorted medium and dark scraps totaling at least 1 3/4 yards
• Assorted light, neutral scraps totaling at least 3 yards
• 1 1/4 yards dark solid, for the borders and binding
• 4 yards backing fabric
• 58" x 70" piece of batting

CUTTING

Pattern pieces are full size and include a 1/4" seam allowance, as do all dimensions given. Try piecing a sample block before cutting fabric for the whole quilt.
• Cut 48: A, light scraps
• Cut 240: A, medium or dark scraps
• Cut 48: B, medium or dark scraps
• Cut 240: B, light scraps
• Cut 96: C, light scraps; or make twenty-four 5 1/2" squares and cut them in quarters diagonally
• Cut 3: 1 5/8" x 44" strips, dark solid, for the borders
• Cut 9: 2" x 44" strips, dark solid, for the borders
• Cut 6: 2 1/2" x 44" strips, dark solid, for the binding

PIECING

• Pick up a light A and a dark B. Fold each piece in half as indicated, creasing the seam allowance of the curve.

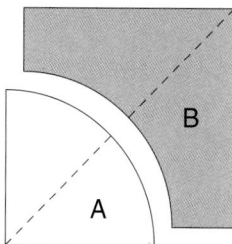

• Place the A and B piece right sides together. Match the creases to align the pieces properly at the center. Pin at the crease.

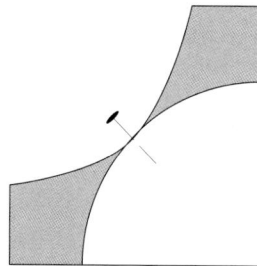

• Now pin the A and B pieces together at both ends of the curved seam. If they bunch up, you have pinned correctly. Now stitch them together along the curve, being careful to align the raw edges of the fabric as you sew, completing the Drunkard's Path square.
NOTE: *Piecing these units by hand offers the quilter a maximum of control. However, many quilters have become adept at machine stitching the curves.*
• Make 48 Drunkard's Path squares with light A's and dark B's. Make 240 Drunkard's Path squares with dark A's and light B's.

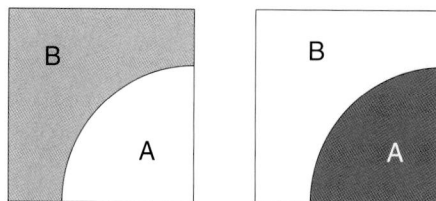

• Take 4 Drunkard's Path squares with light A's and 12 with dark A's. Arrange them as shown, with the light A squares in the corners. Stitch the squares into rows, then join the rows, completing the block. Make 12 blocks.

ASSEMBLY

• Lay out the blocks in 4 horizontal rows of 3. Refer to the photo as needed. Sew the blocks into rows, then join the rows.
• Refer to the mitering section of the *General Directions* as needed. Center and stitch a 2" x 44" dark solid strip to the quilt's top and bottom edges. Start and stop stitching 1/4" from the fabric's edge.
• Take the three 1 5/8" x 44" dark solid strips. Cut one in half and stitch a half to one end of each of the two 44" dark solid strips. Then center and sew these strips to the left and right sides of the quilt. Start and stop stitching 1/4" from the fabric's edge.
• Miter the corners.
NOTE: *Since strips of different widths meet in the corners, you will not have perfect miters. Just do your best.*
• Take 15 Drunkard's Path squares and 15 of the light scrap triangles. Arrange them to form a pieced border unit. You can stitch the squares and triangles together easily by working in diagonal rows. Make a second border unit like the first.

"Drunkard's Path II" by Jo Anne Parisi of West Springfield, Massachusetts. For this attractive scrap quilt, Jo Anne hand pieced 192 Drunkard's Path units into 12-inch blocks. Her clever pieced border, inspired by an antique quilt, features the same units on point.

• Sew the border units to the top and bottom edges of the quilt, positioning each border unit with its longer side touching the dark solid border.

• Take 21 Drunkard's Path squares and 21 light scrap triangles. Arrange them to form a pieced border unit with 12 triangles along the longer side. Stitch the squares and triangles together in diagonal rows. Then make a second border unit like this.

• Sew the border units to the left and right sides of the quilt. Again, position them so that their longer side is against the dark solid border.

• Arrange 6 Drunkard's Path squares and 6 light scrap triangles as shown, then stitch them together, making a corner unit for the border. Make 4 corner units like this. Join one to each corner of the quilt, referring to the photo as needed.

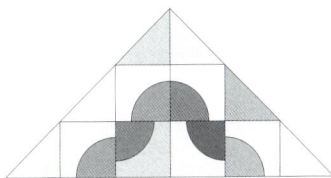

• Take 4 of the 2" x 44" dark solid strips and sew them end to end in pairs. Center and sew these to the left and right sides of the quilt. Start and stop stitching 1/4" from the edge of the fabric.

• Cut a 2" x 44" dark solid strip in half and sew a half to each of the 2 remaining 2" x 44" dark solid strips. Then center and sew these strips to the top and bottom edges of the quilt. Miter the corners.

• Finish the quilt as described in the *General Directions*. Mark the top with your quilting design, as needed. Quiltmaker Jo Anne Parisi used several designs on her top, including a 3/4" diagonal grid and parallel lines spaced only 1/4" apart. Use the 2 1/2" x 44" strips for the binding.❦

Pattern pieces for Drunkard's Path are on page 28.

Elliot's Star Garden

Shimmering colors add excitement to an old-fashioned star pattern.

QUILT SIZE: 44" square
BLOCK SIZE: 6"

MATERIALS

Yardage is estimated for 44" fabric.
- 1 yard bold green floral
- 1/2 yard bold blue floral
- 1 yard dark blue print, for the background
- 3/4 yard medium blue
- 1/4 yard light blue print
- 1/4 yard pale blue
- 1/4 yard deep green
- 1/4 yard medium green
- 1/4 yard pale green
- 1/2 yard lavender
- 2 1/2 yards backing fabric
- 48" square of batting

CUTTING

Pattern pieces are full size and include a 1/4" seam allowance, as do all dimensions given.
- Cut 4: 4 3/4" squares, bold green floral
- Cut 32: A, bold green floral; to cut without templates, make eight 4 1/4" squares, then cut them in quarters diagonally
- Cut 4: 3 1/2" x 44" strips, bold green floral.
NOTE: *These strips are for the outside border. You may need an additional strip if your fabric is not a full 44" wide. However, wait until you are ready to stitch the border before cutting another strip.*
- Cut 5: 4 3/4" squares, bold blue floral
- Cut 40: A, bold blue floral; or make ten 4 1/4" squares, then cut them in quarters diagonally
- Cut 24: B, dark blue; or cut 2 5/8" squares
- Cut 16: C, dark blue; or cut 2" squares
- Cut 40: A, dark blue print; or make ten 4 1/4" squares, then cut them in quarters diagonally
- Cut 4: 3 1/2" squares, dark blue print
- Cut 8: 3 1/2" x 6 1/2" rectangles, dark blue print
- Cut 16: D, dark blue print; or make eight 2 3/8" squares and cut them in half diagonally
- Cut 32: D, light blue print; or make sixteen 2 3/8" squares and cut them in half diagonally
- Cut 4: B, light blue print; or cut 2 5/8" squares
- Cut 16: E, deep green; or make eight 3 7/8" squares and cut them in half diagonally
- Cut 32: A, medium green; or make eight 4 1/4" squares and cut them in quarters diagonally
- Cut 16: B, pale green; or cut 2 5/8" squares
- Cut 20: E, medium blue; or make ten 3 7/8" squares and cut them in half diagonally
- Cut 5: 2 1/2" x 44" strips, medium blue, for the binding
- Cut 40: A, lavender; or make ten 4 1/4" squares and cut them in quarters diagonally
- Cut 20: B, pale blue; or cut 2 5/8" squares
- Cut 2: 1 1/2" x 36 1/2" strips, pale blue, for the inner border
- Cut 2: 1 1/2" x 38 1/2" strips, pale blue, for the inner border

PIECING

Block 1

- Stitch medium blue E triangles to 2 opposite sides of a 4 1/4" bold blue floral square. Then stitch medium blue E's to the other 2 sides.

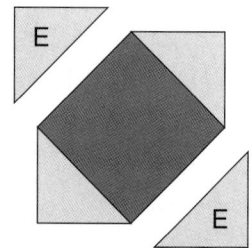

- Make 5 blocks like this. Press and stack the blocks; label them Block 1.

Block 2

- Stitch dark green E triangles to 2 opposite sides of a 4 1/4" bold green floral square, just as you did for Block 1. Then stitch dark green E's to the other 2 sides.
- Make 4 blocks. Press and stack as before, and label them Block 2.

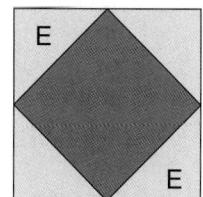

Block 3

- Stitch dark blue print D triangles to 2 opposite sides of a light blue print B. Stitch dark blue print D's to the other 2 sides, completing the block's center unit. Make 4 center units. Press them and set them aside.

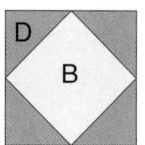

- Stitch light blue print D triangles to the left and right sides of a dark blue print A triangle, as shown, to

Sally Nadelman of New Berlin, New York, made "Elliot's Star Garden" (55" x 55") for her son. She achieved its sparkling transparency effect after taking a color workshop with Judi Warren at Quilting by the Lake. A quiltmaker by profession, Sally is proud to say that this piece was juried into the "Quilts-Art-Quilts" show at Schweinfurth in Auburn, New York. Our pattern on page 14 makes a 44" x 44" wallhanging.

form a Flying Geese unit. Make 16.

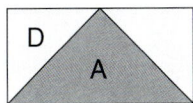

• Using one center unit, 4 Flying Geese units and 4 dark blue print C squares, lay out Block 3 as shown. Stitch the units into 3 rows, then join the rows. Make 4 blocks. Press, stack and label them Block 3.

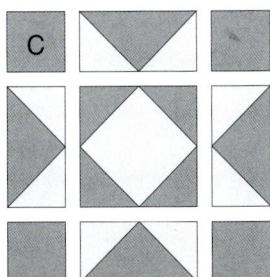

Block 4

• Make a Four Patch using 2 dark blue print B's, 1 pale green B and 1 pale blue B. Arrange the colors as shown. Make 12. Set them aside.

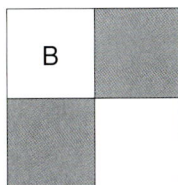

• Stitch lavender A triangles and bold blue floral A triangles in pairs, exactly as shown. Make 20 of each type of pieced triangle. You will need 12 of each for Block 4 and the remainder for other blocks.

• Stitch medium green A triangles and bold green floral A triangles in pairs, exactly as shown. Make 20 of each type of pieced triangle. You will need 12 of each for Block 4 and the remainder for other blocks.

• Pick up one of the Four Patches you set aside. Stitch pieced triangles to it exactly as shown, completing Block 4. Note that the lavender triangles are always adjacent to the pale blue square, while the medium green triangles are always adjacent to the pale

15

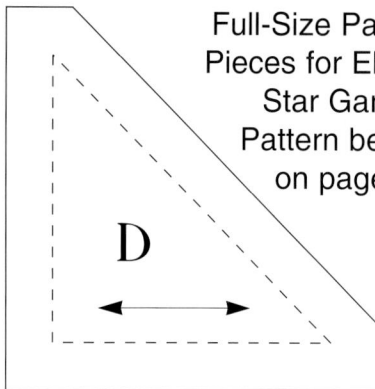

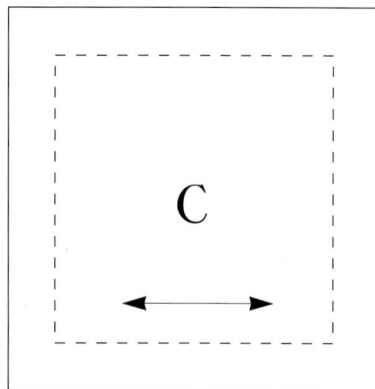

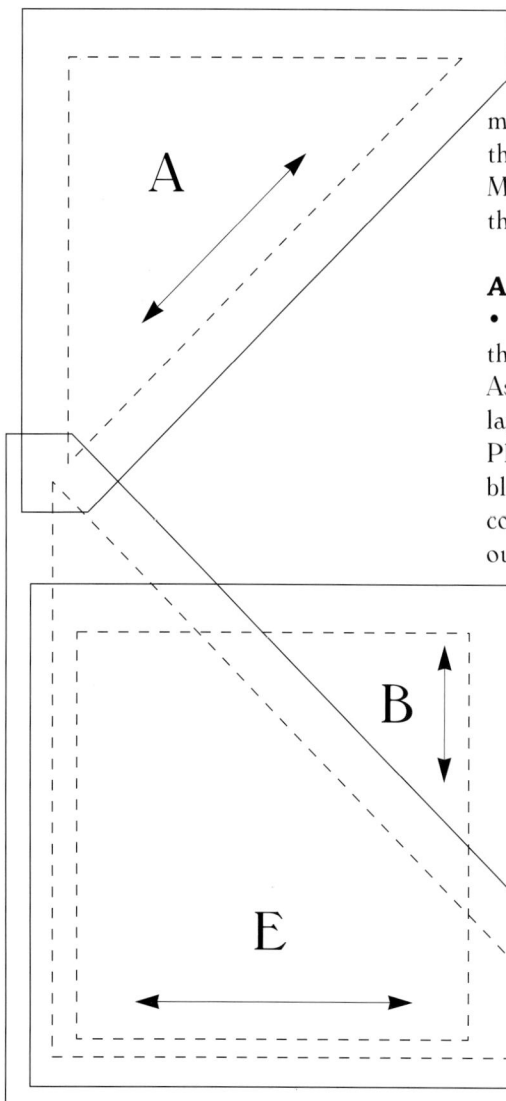

D

C

A

B

E

green square. Make 12 blocks. Press, stack and label them Block 4.

Block 5

• Stitch dark blue print A triangles to 2 adjacent sides of a pale blue B square. Then stitch lavender and blue floral pieced triangles to the left and right sides of this unit, as shown. As you did before, keep the lavender triangles adjacent to the sides of the pale blue square. Make 8 of these units. Press and label them Block 5.

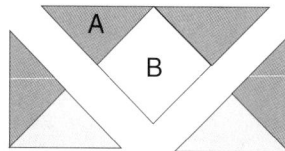

Block 6

• Block 6 is similar to Block 5, but in different colors. Stitch dark blue print A triangles to 2 adjacent sides of a pale green B square. Then stitch medium green and green floral pieced triangles to the left and right sides of this unit. Keep the medium green triangles adjacent to the sides of the pale green square. Make 4 of these units. Press and label them Block 6.

ASSEMBLY

• Referring to the photo and the Assembly Diagram, lay out the blocks. Place a 3 1/2" dark blue square in each corner of the layout. Place the 3 1/2" x 6 1/2" dark blue print rectangles around the sides, in the spaces between Block 6 and

Assembly Diagram

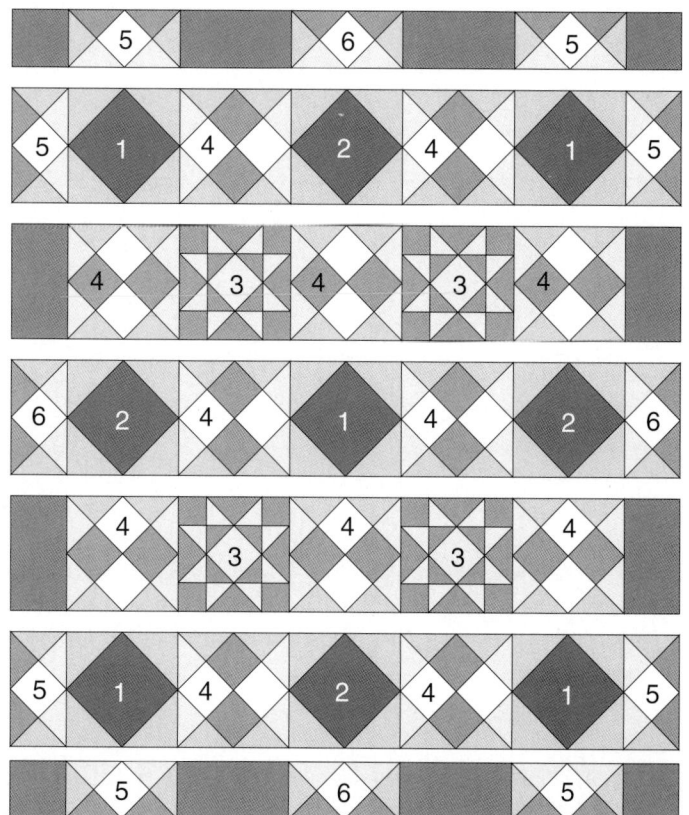

Block 5. Note that in Block 4, the position of the pale blue and pale green squares changes in order to form the blue and green stars.

• Stitch the blocks into rows. Join the rows to complete the quilt top. Press.

• Stitch the 1 1/2" x 36 1/2" pale blue strips to opposite sides of the quilt top.

• Stitch the 1 1/2" x 38 1/2" pale blue strips to the quilt's remaining 2 sides.

• Stitch 3 1/2" x 44" bold green floral strips to 2 opposite sides of the quilt top. Trim the ends of the strips even with the edges of the quilt.

• Measure the width of the quilt at the top and again at the bottom, including the width of the floral border strips you just sewed on. If this measurement is greater than the length of your 2 remaining floral border strips, cut another strip 3 1/2" wide and piece your border strips to the necessary length. Then stitch these strips to the remaining 2 sides of the quilt.

• Finish the quilt as described in the *General Directions*, using the 2 1/2" x 44" strips for the binding.

The Merger

A Log Cabin quilt with a cheerful Pinwheel border.

*Sharyn Craig applied her creative approach to a traditional Barn Raising arrangement of Log Cabin blocks and came up with a quilt she calls **"The Merger."** The 57" square quilt uses a scrappy pinwheel-like border, as well as unusual Log Cabin blocks pieced completely of light-colored fabrics.*

QUILT SIZE: 57" square

BLOCK SIZE

- Log Cabin block: 7" square
- Pinwheel block: 6 1/4" square

MATERIALS

Yardage is estimated for 44" fabric.

- Dark-colored scraps totaling about 1 yard, for the Log Cabin blocks
- Light-colored scraps totaling about 1 1/2 yards, for the Log Cabin blocks
- Brightly colored scraps totaling at least 1 1/8 yards, for the Pinwheel border
- 1/2 yard white or unbleached muslin, for the Pinwheel border
- 1 yard navy, for the Pinwheel border
- 1/4 yard red, for block centers and the inner border
- 1/2 yard red, for piping (or binding, if you prefer)
- 7 yards cotton piping cord (optional)
- 3 1/2 yards backing fabric
- 61" square of batting

CUTTING

Pattern pieces are full size and include a 1/4" seam allowance, as do all dimen-

sions given. After cutting each set of strips, stack them and label the stack with a sticky note.

- Cut 24: 1 1/2" squares, red; label them A
- Cut 48: 1 1/2" squares, light scraps; label them A
- Cut 24: 1 1/2" x 2 1/2" strips, dark scraps; label them B
- Cut 48: 1 1/2" x 2 1/2" strips, light scraps; label them B
- Cut 24: 1 1/2" x 3 1/2" strips, dark scraps; label them C
- Cut 48: 1 1/2" x 3 1/2" strips, light scraps; label them C
- Cut 24: 1 1/2" x 4 1/2" strips, dark scraps; label them D
- Cut 48: 1 1/2" x 4 1/2" strips, light scraps; label them D
- Cut 24: 1 1/2" x 5 1/2" strips, dark scraps; label them E
- Cut 48: 1 1/2" x 5 1/2" strips, light scraps; label them E
- Cut 24: 1 1/2" x 6 1/2" strips, dark scraps; label them F
- Cut 48: 1 1/2" x 6 1/2" strips, light scraps; label them F
- Cut 24: 1 1/2" x 7 1/2" strips, dark scraps; label them G
- Cut 12: 1 1/2" x 7 1/2" strips, light scraps; label them G
- Cut 128: H, navy
- Cut 128: J, bright-colored scraps, in 32 sets of 4 matching pieces
- Cut 128: K, white
- Cut 5: 1 3/8" x 44" strips, red, for the inner border
- Cut 7 yards of 1" bias strips from the 1/2 yard of red fabric; if you're used to cutting a continuous bias strip from a fabric square, start with a 16" square.

NOTE: *This quilt is finished with piping instead of binding. If you prefer a standard binding, cut six 2 1/2" x 44" strips from the red fabric and use them for the binding.*

PIECING
Log Cabin Blocks

- There are two colorations of the Log Cabin block in this quilt—24 of the light and dark blocks, and 12 blocks pieced entirely from light fabrics. We will be piecing both kinds at once in assembly line fashion.
- Chain piecing—running all the pieced units through the sewing machine without clipping the threads between them until afterwards—saves time in a project like this. Sharyn Craig finds that finger pressing is adequate after sewing each step, but feel free to press with an iron if you prefer.
- Begin by joining a red A piece to light A piece. Make 24 units like this. Join the remaining 24 light A's in pairs, as shown.

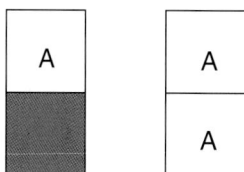

- Take 36 light B pieces and join one to each of the pieced units.

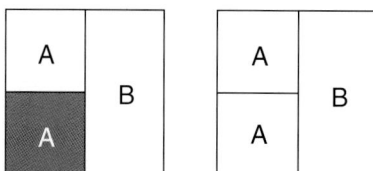

- Take the 24 dark B pieces and join them to the 24 units with red centers. Then take the remaining 12 light B pieces and join them to the all-light pieced units.

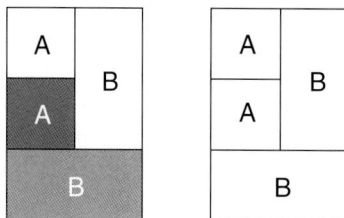

- Take the 24 dark C pieces and join them to the 24 units with red centers. Then join 12 of the light C's to the all-light pieced units.

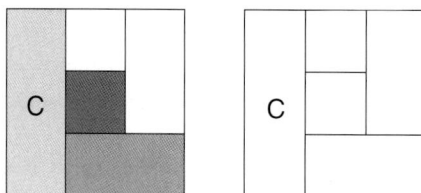

- Taking the remaining light C pieces and join one to each of the pieced units.

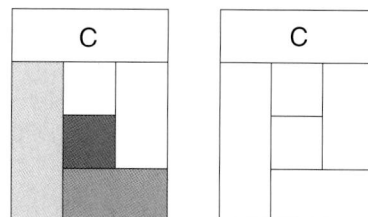

- Take 36 light D pieces and join one to each of the pieced units.

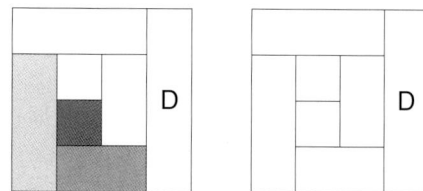

- Take 24 dark D pieces and join one to each of the pieced units with a red center. Then take the remaining 12 light D's and join one to each of the all-light units.

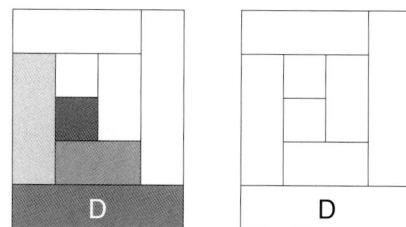

- Continuing in the same manner, take 24 dark E pieces and join one to each of the pieced units with a red center. Then take 12 light E pieces and join one to each of the all-light pieced units.
- Take the remaining 36 light E pieces and join one to each of the pieced units.
- Take 36 light F pieces and join one to each of the 36 pieced units.
- Take the 24 dark F pieces. Join one to each of the pieced units with a red center. Then take the 12 remaining light F pieces and join one to each of the all-light blocks.
- Take the 24 dark G pieces. Join one to each of the pieced units with a red center. Then take the 12 light G pieces and join one to each of the all-light blocks.
- You have now completed all 36 Log Cabin blocks. 24 will be as shown and 12 will be light colored all over. Press them lightly, being careful not to stretch them.

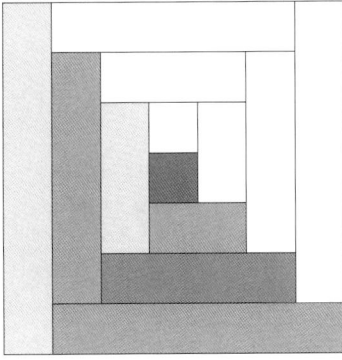

- Referring to the photo as needed, arrange the Log Cabin blocks in 6 rows of 6. Stitch the blocks into rows, then join the rows, matching seams.
- Stitch 1 3/8" x 44" red strips to 2 opposite sides of the quilt. Trim the excess length from the strips.
- Stitch the other three 1 3/8" x 44" strips end to end. Cut the resulting long strip in half. Stitch the halves to the quilt's 2 remaining sides. Trim.

Pinwheel Blocks

- Take 4 navy H pieces, 4 matching J pieces and 4 white K pieces. Join them to make 4 of the pieced triangles illustrated.

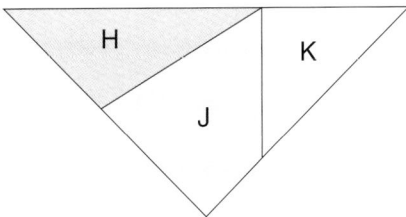

- Join the 4 pieced triangles to make the Pinwheel block illustrated. Make 32.

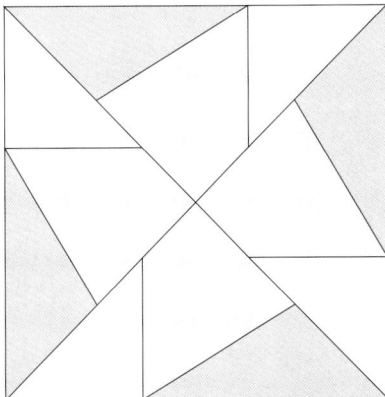

- Press the blocks carefully to avoid stretching them.

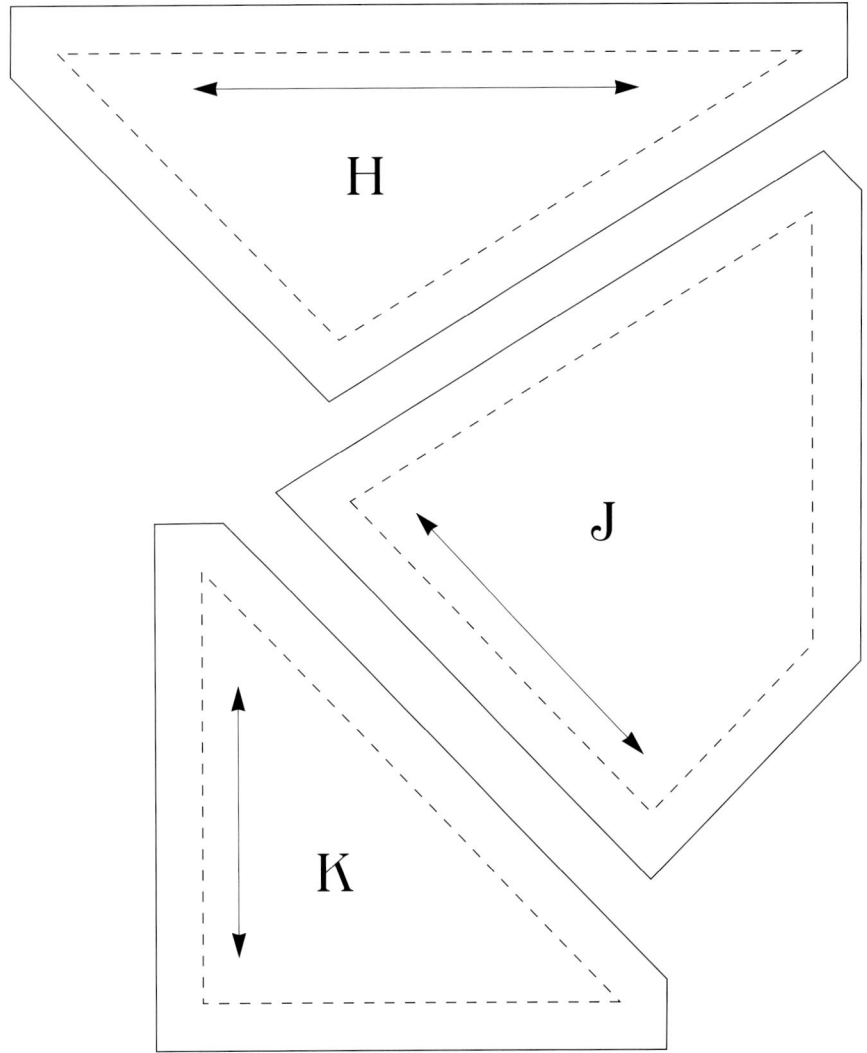

Full-Size Pattern Pieces for The Merger
Pattern begins on page 17.

- Make 2 border rows with 7 Pinwheel blocks in each. Join them to 2 opposite sides of the quilt.
- Make 2 border rows with 9 Pinwheel blocks in each. Join them to the remaining sides of the quilt. Press.

Finishing

- Make 7 yards of red piping by stitching the cotton piping cord inside the 1" red bias strip you prepared.
- Lay out the quilt top right side up. Position the piping along the outer edge of the quilt top, so that the raw edges of the piping and quilt top are even. Start with one side and pin the piping in place on that side only.
- Stitch just 2 or 3 inches of piping to the quilt top. Stop and flip the raw edge of the piping under the quilt, to see how it will look. You may want to adjust the width of the seam you are making, or the placement of the piping along the outer edge of the quilt top.
- Continue sewing the piping to the quilt top, rounding the corners slightly, as needed.
- Layer the backing, batting and finished quilt top together and baste for quilting. Quilt as desired.
- To finish the edges, turn the quilt right side down. Then turning the raw edges of the backing inside the quilt, blindstitch the quilt backing to the piping, being careful to cover the stitching line. ❦

19

Delectable Appalachians

Bright scraps make this traditional pattern not only delectable, but fun!

"Delectable Appalachians" (82" x 100") by Patricia Mullins Gabriel of Conover, North Carolina. Friends and relatives scoured the country from coast to coast to find enough red, orange and yellow fabrics for this beautifully scrappy quilt—all 3,930 pieces! Trish gives inspiration credit to Darra Duffy Williamson's quilt "Appalachian Spring."

QUILT SIZE: 81 3/8" x 99"
BLOCK SIZE: 5" square

MATERIALS

Yardage is estimated for 44" fabric.
- A wide variety of print scraps in the colors shown—or your choice of colors—totaling 12 to 13 yards. Be sure to include darks, mediums and lights.
- 1 1/4 yards red, for the inner border and binding
- 6 yards backing fabric
- 86" x 104" piece of batting

CUTTING

All dimensions given include 1/4" seam allowance.
- Cut 1,500: 2 1/8" squares, assorted scraps; half (750) should be light to medium and half medium to dark. Cut them in half diagonally to yield 3,000 triangles. Label them A.
- Cut 12: 8 3/8" squares, assorted scraps; cut them from corner to corner in both directions making 44 setting triangles for the sides of the quilt; stack and label them.
- Cut 300: 1 3/4" squares, light to medium scraps. Label them B.
- Cut 150: 3 3/8" squares, assorted scraps; cut them in half diagonally to yield 300 triangles. Label them C.
- Cut 126: 5 7/8" squares, assorted scraps; cut them in half diagonally to yield 252 triangles. Label them D.
- Cut 2: 6 9/16" squares, scraps; cut them in quarters diagonally, making 8 triangles; label them E. You'll need 4.
- Cut 5: 2 5/8" x 44" strips, red
- Cut 4: 1 1/2" x 44" strips, red
- Cut 9: 2 1/2" x 44" strips, red, for the binding

PIECING

- Stitch 2 A's together to yield a pieced square. Make 4 pieced squares in this manner. Vary your color placement, always keeping one half darker than the other for contrast.
- Stitch 2 pairs of pieced squares, positioning them as shown.

- Stitch an A triangle and a B square to one of the pairs and an A triangle to the other pair. Make sure your pieces are positioned correctly before you sew.

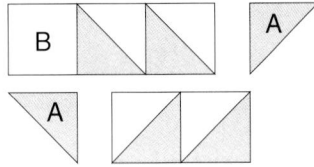

- Stitch the shorter pieced unit to one side of a C triangle. Then sew the

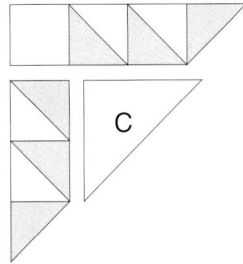

longer pieced unit to the adjacent side of C, completing a pieced triangle as shown. Make 300. When arranging colors, note that some of the blocks in the quilt have high contrast while others have minimal contrast.
- Stitch a D triangle to 252 of the pieced triangles, making completed blocks. Save the remaining 48 pieced triangles, or half-blocks, for the border.

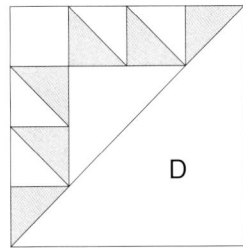

- Lay out your blocks in 18 horizontal rows of 14. The blocks in the original quilt are positioned in groups of 4, as shown in the diagram. Arrange them that way, or any way you prefer. Rearrange individual blocks until you are happy with the color placement. Refer to the photo for guidance

and inspiration. Remember—this is your quilt.
- Stitch your blocks into rows. Then join the rows to complete the interior of the quilt top. Press the top.
- Join 4 of the 2 5/8" x 44" red strips in pairs, end to end. Cut the remaining 2 5/8" red strip in half and sew a half to each of the paired strips. Sew the resulting 2 long red strips to the quilt's 2 longer sides. Trim the ends of the strips as needed.
- Join the 1 1/2" x 44" red strips in pairs, end to end. Sew the paired strips to the top and bottom edges of the quilt. Trim the ends.
- Use the remaining 48 half-blocks, 48 setting triangles and 4 E triangles for the outer border. Make 2 border rows, each with 13 half-blocks and 14 setting triangles, arranging them as shown. Center and stitch them to the quilt's long sides.

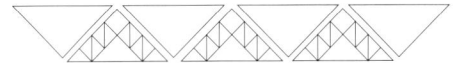

- Take 3 half-blocks. Referring to the diagram as needed, remove one small triangle from one end of 2 half-blocks. Join these half-blocks and 2 E triangles as indicated. Use this pieced unit as the center of a border row, adding 4 half-blocks and 5 setting triangles to both the left and the right sides. Make a second border row like the first.

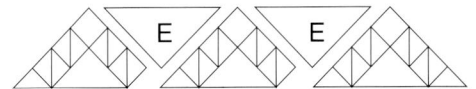

- Center and stitch the border rows to the top and bottom edges of the quilt. Then sew the diagonal seams at the corners of the border.
- Finish the quilt as described in the *General Directions*, using the 2 1/2" x 44" strips for the binding. ❦

Amish Window

A stunning Shoo Fly quilt!

QUILT SIZE: 41" x 92"
BLOCK SIZE: 6" square

MATERIALS

Yardage is estimated for 44" fabric.

• Fabric scraps in solid colors—shades of pink, blue, green and purple
NOTE: *To achieve the look of the quilt in the photograph, there should be several greens, several pinks, etc. The colors should vary both in shade and intensity. The shade is determined by the amount of white, making the color lighter or darker. The intensity is determined by the amount of gray, making it brighter or more subdued.*

• 3 yards black solid, for the background, outer border and binding
• 3/8 yard pink or other solid color, for the inner border; the border color should echo one of the colors used in the pieced portion of the quilt
• 3 yards backing fabric
• 45" x 96" piece of batting

CUTTING

Pattern pieces are full size and include a 1/4" seam allowance, as do all dimensions given. We recommend making a sample block before cutting fabric for the whole quilt.

For each of the 39 blocks:

• Cut 4: matching A triangles, solid scraps; or cut two 2 7/8" squares in half diagonally
• Cut 4: matching B squares, same solid fabric as the A's; or cut 2 1/2" squares
NOTE: *It would be in accordance with Amish quiltmaking practice to use two almost matching solids in a single block. Even if you don't run out of a given fabric, a mixture like this in sever-al blocks would give an interesting effect.*

In addition:

• Cut 156: A, black; or cut seventy-eight 2 7/8" squares in half diagonally
• Cut 39: B, black; or cut 2 1/2" squares
• Cut 2: 13 5/8" squares, black; then cut each in half diagonally, making 4 large corner triangles
• Cut 3: 9 3/4" squares, black; then cut them in quarters diagonally, making setting triangles for the edges of the quilt
• Cut 6: 2" x 44" strips, pink, for the inner border
• Cut 6: 6 1/2" x 44" strips, black, for the outer border
• Cut 8: 2 1/2" x 44" strips, black, for the binding

PIECING

• Take the matching scrap A and B pieces for a single pieced block—4 A triangles and 4 B squares from a single fabric. In addition, take 4 black A triangles and a black B square. Join the scrap A's to the black A's, making 4 pieced squares like the one shown.

• Stitch the pieced squares, the black square and the colored squares into 3 rows, as shown. Then join the rows, matching seams, to complete a Shoo Fly block. Make 39.

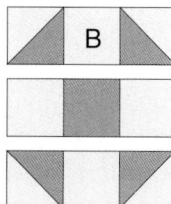

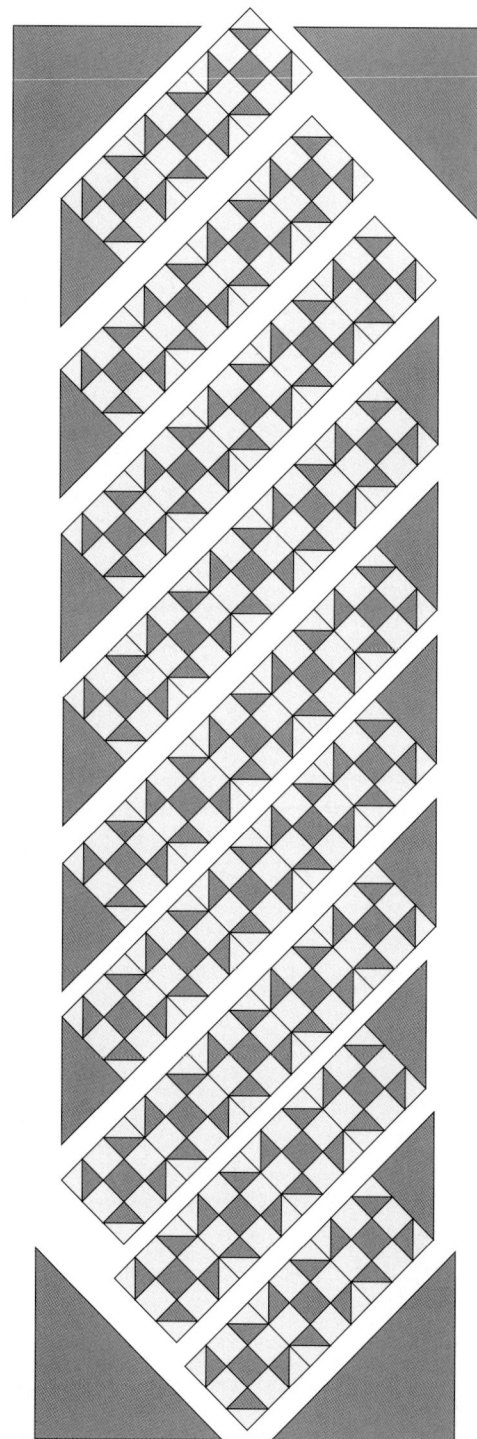

Pamela Berg of Madison, Wisconsin, calls this luminous creation **"Amish Window"** *(41" x 92"). Indeed, the old-fashioned Shoo Fly blocks glow as if they were cut from pieces of colored glass. Collect some pretty solid-colored fabrics and light up a room with your own version of this quilt.*

ASSEMBLY

• Referring to the Assembly Diagram as needed, lay out the 39 pieced blocks on point. Place the 12 black setting triangles in the spaces along the edges of the layout. Move the pieced blocks around until you achieve an interesting color arrangement.

• Stitch the blocks and setting triangles into diagonal rows. Then join the rows, matching seams.

• Stitch a large black corner triangle to each corner of the quilt.

• Take 4 of the 2" x 44" pink strips and join them in pairs, end to end making long strips. Sew one long strip to each of the quilt's long sides. Trim the ends of the strips even with the quilt's top and bottom edges.

• Sew the remaining two 2" x 44" pink strips to the top and bottom edges of the quilt. Trim the ends of the strips.

• Add the outer border in the same way, using the 6 1/2" x 44" black strips.

• Finish the quilt as described in the *General Directions*, using the 2 1/2" x 44" strips for the binding. ❦

Full-Size Pattern
Pieces for
Amish
Window

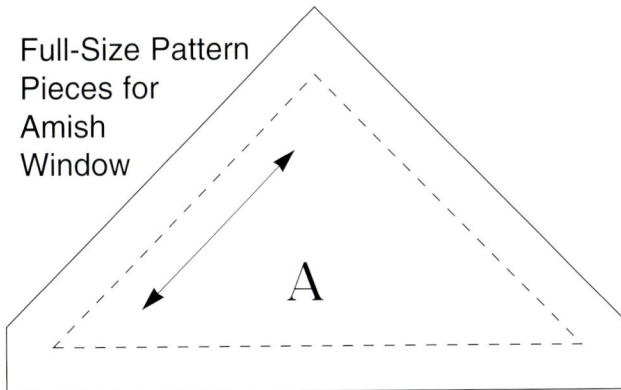

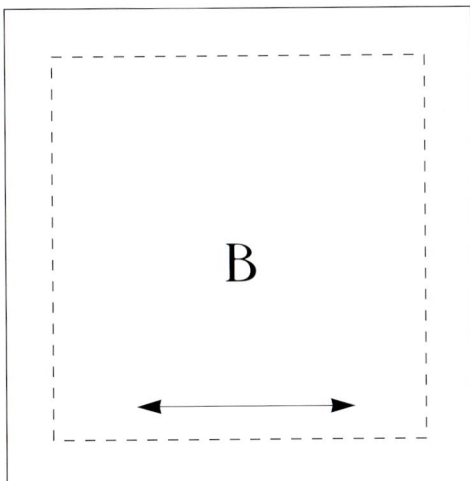

A

B

Shared Pleasures

A snappy, scrappy quilt in the time-honored Buckeye Beauty pattern!

QUILT SIZE: 84" x 96"
BLOCK SIZE: 12" square

MATERIALS

Yardage is estimated for 44" fabric.
• Light to medium scraps totaling at least 1 7/8 yards
• Medium to dark scraps totaling at least 1 7/8 yards
• Medium scraps totaling at least 1 yard
• Dark scraps totaling at least 1 yard
• 2 5/8 yards light-colored print, for the background and inner border
• 2 7/8 yards medium or dark fabric, for the outer border
• 7/8 yard fabric for the binding
• 7 1/2 yards backing fabric
NOTE: *This yardage will be adequate if you make the backing in 3 strips with horizontal seams. For 3 strips with vertical seams (i.e. parallel to the length of the quilt), you'll need 8 1/2 yards.*

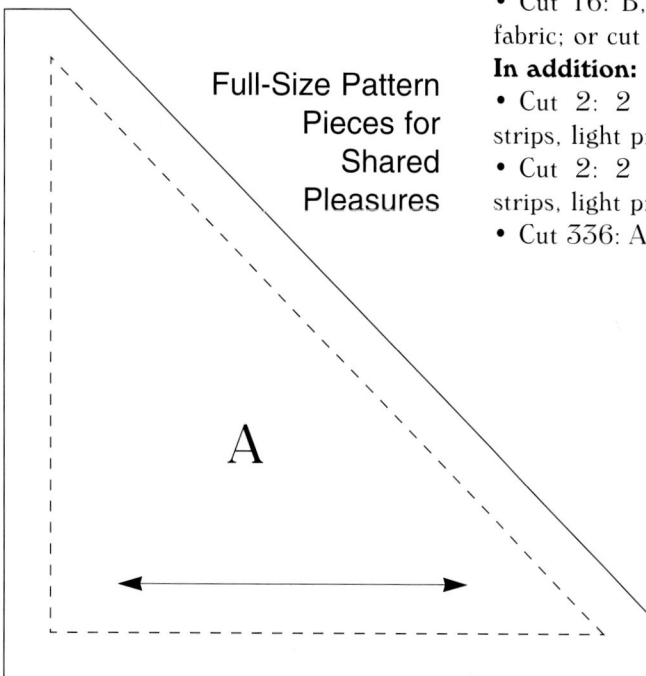

Full-Size Pattern Pieces for Shared Pleasures

A

• 88" x 100" piece of batting

CUTTING

Pattern pieces are full size and include a 1/4" seam allowance, as do all dimensions given. We recommend making a sample block before cutting fabric for the whole quilt. Be sure to cut the lengthwise strips parallel to the selvage before cutting the A pieces from the light fabric.

For each of the 42 blocks:
NOTE: *Each block uses 4 different fabrics in addition to the light background fabric.*
• Cut 4: A, dark scrap fabric; or cut two 3 7/8" squares in half diagonally, making 4 triangles
• Cut 4: A, medium scrap fabric; or cut two 3 7/8" squares in half diagonally
• Cut 16: B, medium to dark scrap fabric; or cut 2" squares
• Cut 16: B, light to medium scrap fabric; or cut 2" squares
In addition:
• Cut 2: 2 1/2" x 80" lengthwise strips, light print
• Cut 2: 2 1/2" x 92" lengthwise strips, light print
• Cut 336: A, light print; or cut 168

B

squares measuring 3 7/8", then cut them in half diagonally
• Cut 2: 4 1/2" x 88" lengthwise strips, fabric for the outer border
• Cut 2: 4 1/2" x 100" lengthwise strips, fabric for the outer border
• Cut 9: 2 1/2" x 44" strips, fabric for the binding

PIECING

• Take the medium and dark pieces for a single block, along with 8 light A triangles. Sew each medium A and each dark A to a light A, making 8 pieced squares.

• Stitch each medium B to a dark B. Then join the pairs to make Four Patches. Make 8 Four Patches for each block.

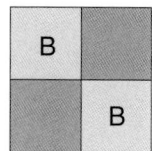

• Take 2 Four Patches and 2 pieced squares—one of each kind. Join them to make a quarter of the block. Make 4 identical quarters.

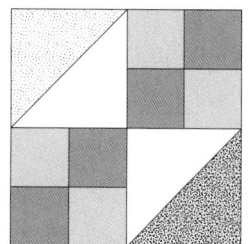

*Doris Thackrah of Wilmington, Delaware, stitched **"Shared Pleasures"** (84" x 96") with her friend Philippa Lammey. She explains, "Philippa and I made two of each block, then traded one. We ended up with the same blocks. We set our quilts differently and quilted them differently. It was a fun experience!" Old-fashioned Buckeye Beauty blocks and ordinary fabric scraps have teamed up here for a truly eye-catching quilt.*

ASSEMBLY

• Lay out the blocks in 7 horizontal rows of 6. You may want to rearrange the blocks in order to balance the colors.

• Join the quarters to form the block. Make 42 blocks.

• When you are happy with the arrangement, stitch the blocks into rows, then join the rows, matching seams.

• Refer to the mitering section of the *General Directions*, as needed.

• Fold each 2 1/2" x 80" light print strip end to end, creasing to mark the center. Fold and crease each 4 1/2" x 88" strip of fabric for the outer border in the same way. Then match the creases to center a shorter strip on a longer one. Stitch them together along their length, right sides together.

Press the seams toward the darker fabric. Make 2. Stitch these strips to the top and bottom edges of the quilt. Begin and end your stitching 1/4" from the fabric's edge.

• Join the 2 1/2" x 92" light print strips to the 4 1/2" x 100" outer border strips in the same way. Stitch these strips to the right and left sides of the quilt.

• Miter the corners of the border.

• Finish the quilt as described in the *General Directions*, using the 2 1/2" x 44" strips for the binding. ❦

Expanding Universe

Strip piece this handsome Broken Star quilt in record time!

"Expanding Universe" (87" x 87") by Lynda Carswell of San Francisco, California. Although she works full-time as a registered nurse, Lynda found enough free moments to stitch this striking Broken Star quilt as a wedding present for her son, Jeremy Meyer. Her masterful use of stark black and white adds graphic emphasis and drama to this old-time pattern. Lynda used cotton flannel for the backing, "to make it more snuggly and keep it in place on the bed."

QUILT SIZE: 87" square

MATERIALS

Yardage is estimated for 44" fabric.
- 1 1/4 yards black
- 1 1/4 yards white
- 3 3/4 yards blue, for the background
- 2 1/2 yards red, for the borders
- 3/4 yard dark fabric, for the binding
- 7 3/4 yards backing fabric
- 91" square of batting
- Rotary cutter, mat and plastic ruler with a marked 45° angle

CUTTING

All dimensions include a 1/4" seam allowance. You may wish to make one or 2 of the large pieced diamonds as practice before cutting fabric for the whole quilt. Cut the lengthwise strips parallel to the selvage before cutting any other pieces from the red and blue fabrics.

- Cut 16: 2 1/8" x 44" strips, black
- Cut 16: 2 1/8" x 44" strips, white
- Cut 4: lengthwise strips 5" x 92", blue, for the outer border

- Cut 12: 9 3/4" squares, blue
- Cut 4: 9 3/4" x 19" rectangles, blue
- Cut 2: 14 1/4" squares, blue; then cut them in half diagonally, making 8 setting triangles
- Cut 4: lengthwise strips 2 1/8" x 72", red, for the inner red border
- Cut 4: lengthwise strips 2 1/4" x 84", red, for the outer red border
- Cut 152: A, red
- Cut 304: B, blue
- Cut 4: 4 3/4" x 13" strips, blue
- Cut 9: 2 1/2" x 44" strips, binding fabric

PIECING THE DIAMONDS

- Use 1/4" seams throughout.
- Take two 2 1/8" x 44" black strips and two 2 1/8" x 44" white strips. Sew them together, alternating the colors, and placing each strip about 1 1/2" lower than its neighbor.

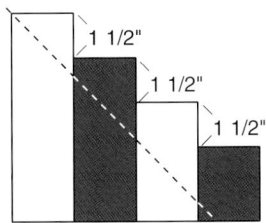

Make 8 of these pieced sets of strips, or "strip sets." Press all the seams toward the black fabric. Then use the 45° of your quilter's ruler to trim off the uneven top edge of the strip set, as indicated.

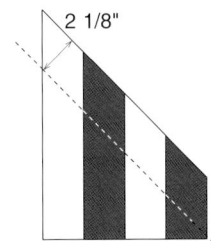

- Placing your quilter's ruler parallel to the angled cut at the top of the strip set, cut a 2 1/8" slice like the one shown.
- Cut a second 2 1/8" slice. Then use your ruler's 45° angle to check the angled cut at the top of the strip set. Trim, if necessary, then cut another 2 1/8" slice. Continue cutting slices, checking the angle after every second slice. Make 128 slices.
- Lay out 4 slices, as shown. Note that the slices are reversible; turning them end to end changes the position of white and black diamonds. Stitch the slices together, matching seams to make a pieced diamond. Note that

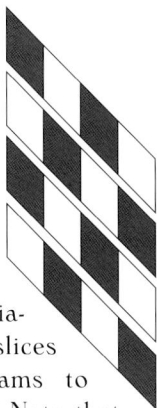

both ends of the diamond are black. You will need 20 pieced diamonds as shown in previous diagram.

- Lay out 4 more slices as shown, then stitch them together making a pieced diamond with white ends. You will need 12 pieced diamonds like this.

ASSEMBLY

- Take 8 of the pieced diamonds with black ends. Lay them out in an 8-pointed star like the one at the center of the quilt. Stitch the pieced diamonds together in pairs. Sew the pairs into half-stars. Then sew the halves together, completing the quilt's center star.
- Stitch a 9 3/4" blue square into each of the spaces between the points of the center star. Sew from the inside toward the outside edge, as indicated by the arrows.

- Sew the remaining pieced diamonds together in threes, making "fans." You will need 4 fans with white ends and 4 fans with black ends.

- Referring to the Assembly Diagram on page 28, stitch the fans into the spaces between the 9 3/4" blue squares. Stitch from the center out-

ward. Sew the fans to the blue squares first, then sew the seams joining the fans to adjacent fans as shown in the Assembly Diagram on the following page.

- Following the diagram, lay the remaining four 9 3/4" blue squares, the four 9 3/4" x 19" blue rectangles and the 8 blue setting triangles in the spaces around the fans. Sew from the center outward. Press the quilt top.

BORDERS

- Stitch together 38 A's and 74 B's in the manner indicated, making a pieced border row. There will be A's at both ends of the row. Make 4 identical pieced border rows.

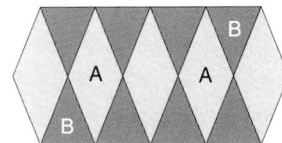

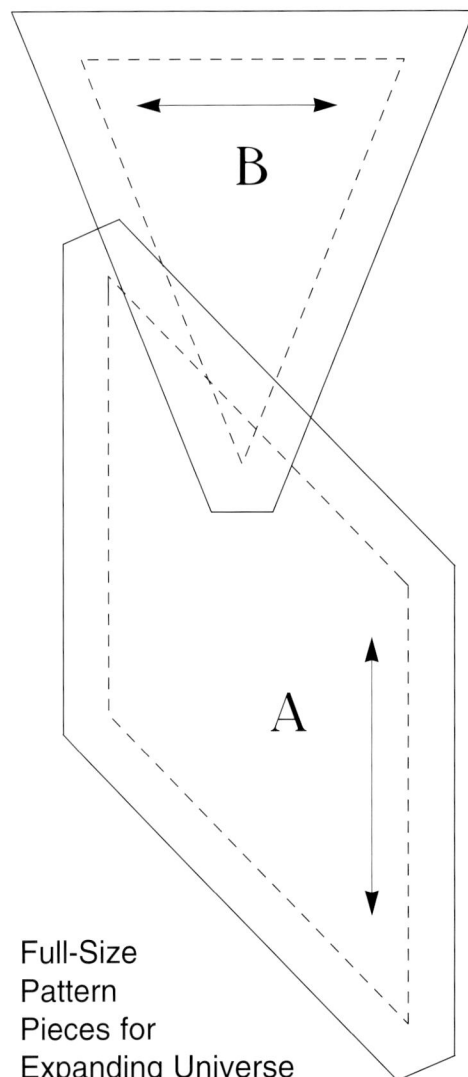

Full-Size
Pattern
Pieces for
Expanding Universe

• Fold the 4 3⁄4" x 13" blue strips end to end, creasing to mark the center. Use your ruler's 45° angle to make the diagonal cut shown. Position the ruler so that the cut falls roughly at the center of the crease. Cutting one strip yields 2 trapezoids for the ends of a pieced border row. Cut 8 trapezoids.

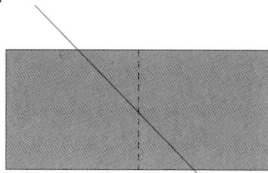

• Add B pieces and trapezoids to the ends of each pieced border row, as shown.

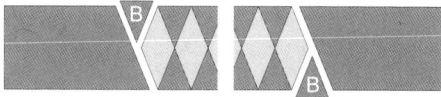

• Center and stitch a 2 1⁄8" x 72" red strip to the lower edge of a pieced border row. You can find the center of your strips by folding them end to end and creasing. Then match the creases. Center and stitch a 2 1⁄4" x 84" red strip to the upper edge of the same pieced border row. Then center and stitch a 5" x 92" blue strip to the upper edge of the 84" red strip. This completes one border unit. Make 4.

• Refer to the mitering instructions in the *General Directions*. Then center a border unit on each side of the quilt center. Consult the photo for correct placement—you want the blue border on the outside edge of the finished quilt. Stitch the borders to the quilt, beginning and ending each line of stitches 1⁄4" from the edge of the fabric.

• Miter the corners of the borders.

• Finish the quilt as described in the *General Directions*, using the 2 1⁄2" x 44" strips for the binding.

Assembly Diagram

Full-Size Pattern Pieces for Drunkard's Path. Pattern begins on page 12.

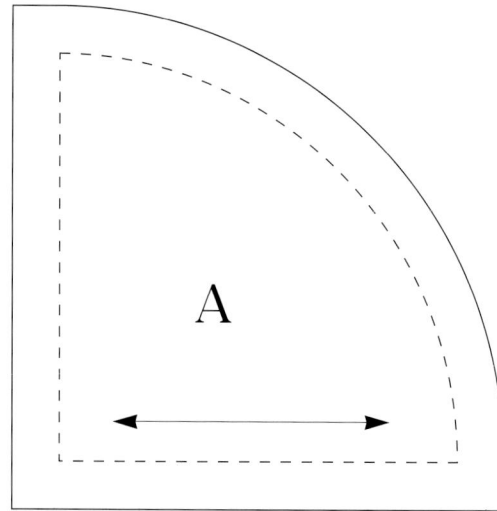

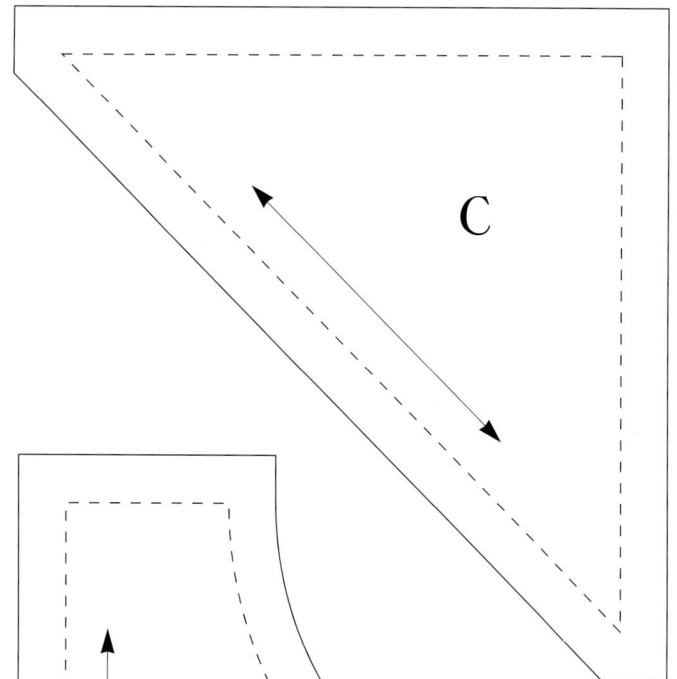

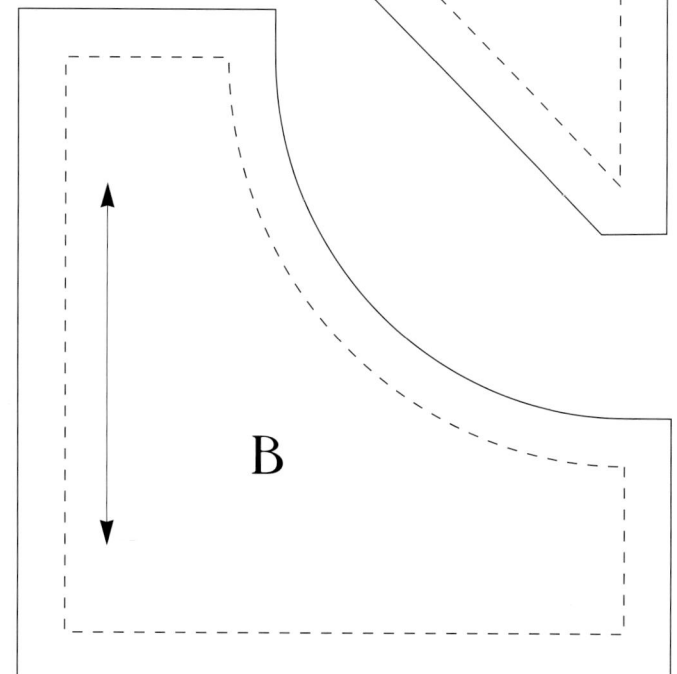

A

C

B

Delectable Mountain Star

This old-time block makes an elegant scrap quilt!

*Pauline Warren's exciting "**Delectable Mountain Star**" quilt (81" x 81") began with the familiar Delectable Mountain block. "I wanted to take a traditional pattern and put it together in a unique way," she explains. "I used up some large prints I thought were 'ugly.' They look pretty good to me now!" To achieve the new look, Pauline set her blocks on point. Half-blocks fill the edges.*

QUILT SIZE: 85" square
BLOCK SIZE: 7 1/2" square

MATERIALS

Yardage is estimated for 44" fabric.
- Medium and dark scraps for the blocks, totaling 3 3/4 to 4 yards
- 6 yards of white, off-white or tan
- 3/4 yard fabric for the binding
- 7 1/2 yards backing fabric

NOTE: *7 1/2 yards of backing will give you a backing pieced in 3 strips of equal width. If you don't mind piecing a narrow strip to go between your 44" strip of backing, 5 1/2 yards will do.*
- 89" square of batting

CUTTING

Pattern pieces are full size and include a 1/4" seam allowance, as do all dimensions given. We recommend making a sample block before cutting fabric for the whole quilt.
- Cut 1,120: A, medium or dark scraps, in sets of 8 matching pieces: to cut without a template, make 2 3/8" squares and cut them in half diagonally—4 squares will yield 8 A's
- Cut 140: C, assorted medium and dark scraps; or make seventy 5 3/8" squares and cut them in half diagonally

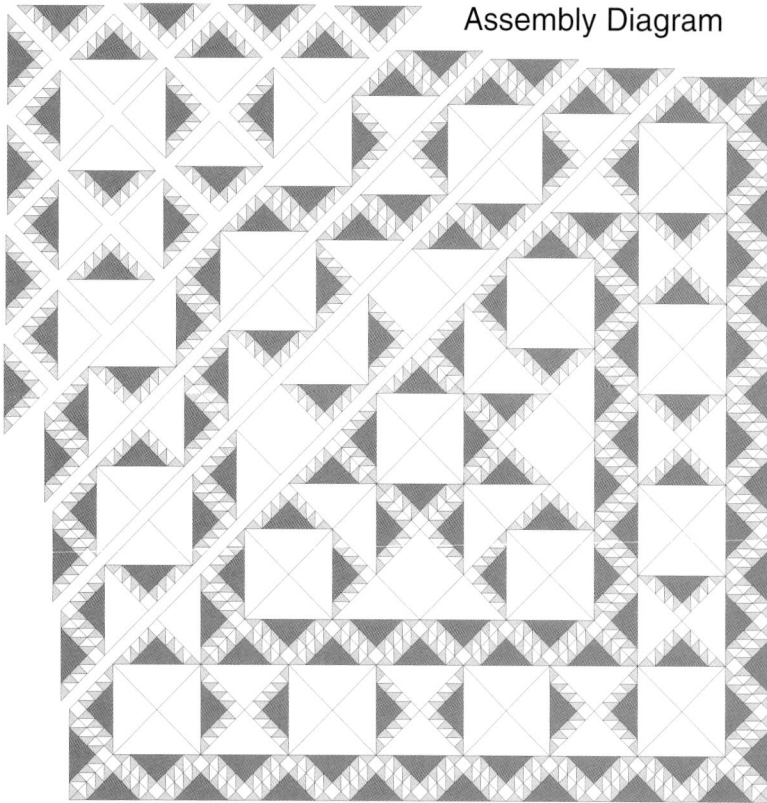

Assembly Diagram

needed, lay out the blocks on point. Note the placement of the four 8" white squares around the center star. Place the half-blocks in the triangular spaces around the edges of the quilt.

• Assemble the quilt in diagonal rows. Join the blocks and half-blocks in each row. Then join the rows, carefully matching the seams.

• Finish the quilt as described in the *General Directions*. Quiltmaker Pauline Warren quilted feather wreaths in the large white spaces. Use the 2 1/2" x 44" strips for the binding. ❧

Full-Size Pattern Pieces for Delectable Mountain Star Pattern begins on page 29.

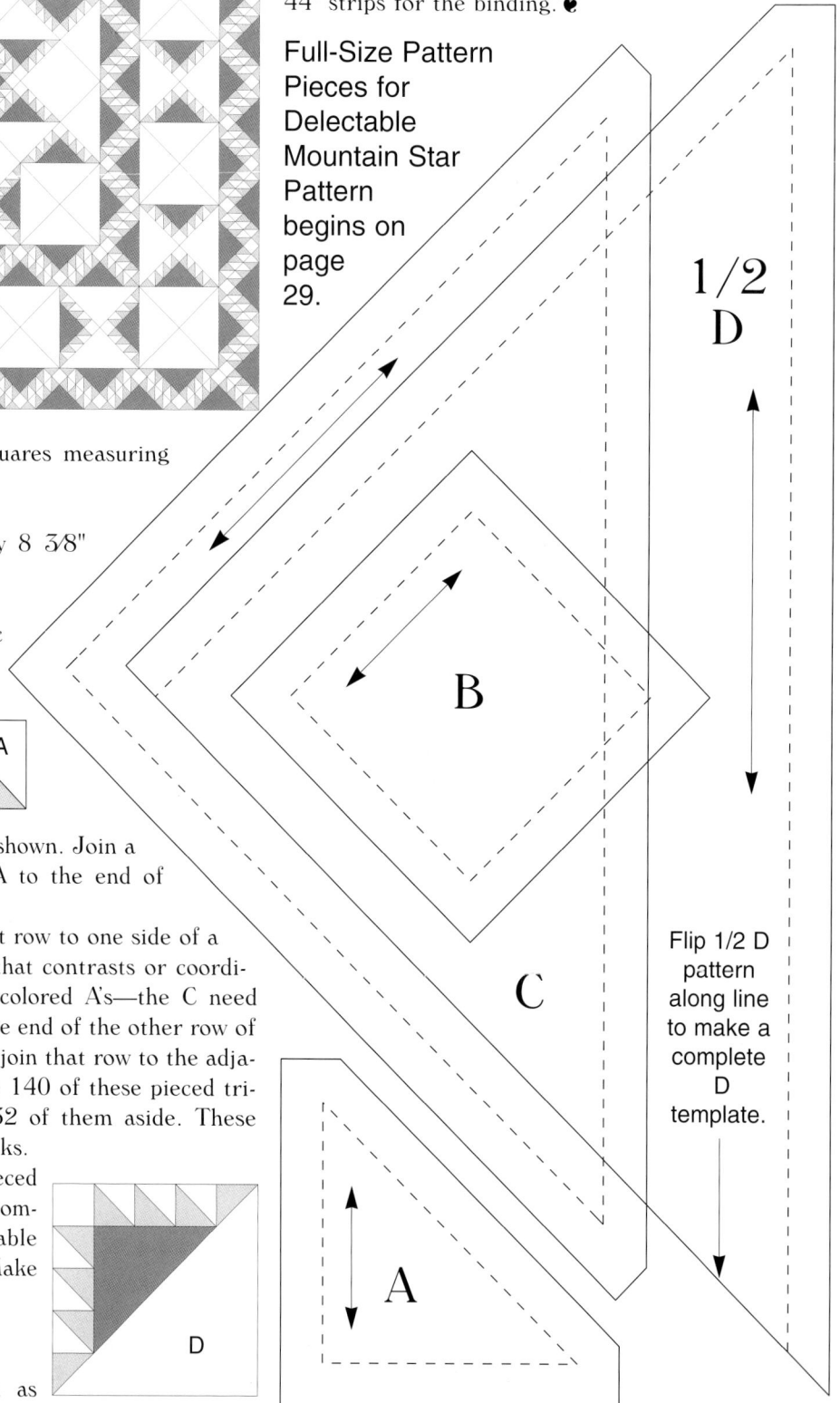

• Cut 840: A, white; or make 420 squares measuring 2 3/8" and cut them in half diagonally
• Cut 140: B, white, or cut 2" squares
• Cut 140: D, white; or make seventy 8 3/8" squares and cut them in half diagonally
• Cut 4: 8" squares, white
• Cut 9: 2 1/2" x 44" strips, binding fabric

PIECING

• Take 8 matching A's. Stitch 6 of them to white A's, making pieced squares.
• Stitch the pieced squares into 2 rows exactly as shown. Join a single colored A to the end of each row.
• Sew the first row to one side of a C. Choose a C that contrasts or coordinates with the colored A's—the C need not match the A's. Stitch a B square to one end of the other row of pieced squares, then join that row to the adjacent side of C. Make 140 of these pieced triangular units. Set 32 of them aside. These will be your half-blocks.
• Join a D to a pieced triangular unit to complete the Delectable Mountain block. Make 108 blocks.

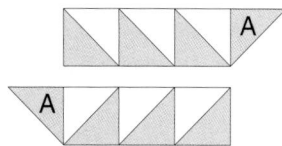

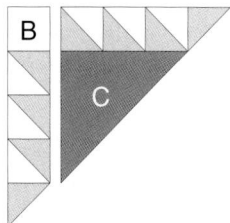

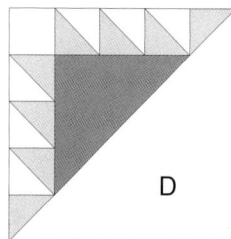

ASSEMBLY

• Referring to the Assembly Diagram as

1/2 D

B

C

A

Flip 1/2 D pattern along line to make a complete D template.

Fan-cy up my Christmas Spirit

A gorgeous Grandmother's Fan quilt!

Cindy Lou Lewis Van Deventer has been making quilts for about 25 years—but has taken "a more serious approach" in recent years. With its richly colored fabrics, **"Fan-cy up my Christmas Spirit"** (76" x 88") is her holiday statement. It was machine pieced and machine quilted.

QUILT SIZE:
76" x 88"

BLOCK SIZE:
12" square

MATERIALS
Yardage is estimated for 44" fabric.
• 1/2 yard each of 8 different red or green fabrics—or use scraps
• 3 3/4 yards

white, for the background squares
- 3/8 yard green print, for the inner border
- 3/8 yard plaid, for the second border
- 1/4 yard red print for the third border
- 1 1/2 yards large-scale Christmas print for outermost border.

NOTE: *You may want to plan on using some of your border fabrics in the pieced fans, as quiltmaker Cindy Van Deventer did.*
- 5/8 yard fabric for the binding—Cindy chose a dark solid
- 5 1/4 yards backing fabric
- 80" x 92" piece of batting

CUTTING

The pattern piece is full size and includes a 1/4" seam allowance, as do all dimensions given. We recommend making a sample block before cutting fabric for the whole quilt.
- Cut 240: A—either cut 30 each from 8 different fabrics as Cindy did, or cut a random mixture
- Cut 30: 12 1/2" squares, white
- Cut 7: 1 1/2" x 44" strips, green print
- Cut 8: 1 1/2" x 44" strips, plaid
- Cut 8: 1" x 44" strips, red print
- Cut 8: 6" x 44" strips, large-scale Christmas print
- Cut 8: 2 1/2" x 44" strips, binding fabric

SEWING

- If you are using just 8 fabrics in your fans, pick up one A piece from each fabric. Decide whether or not you want them to appear in the same position in each block. Then stitch the 8 A's together in the order you chose, to form a fan. Press all the seams in the same direction. Make 30 fans.
- Place a fan on a 12 1/2" white square so that the straight sides of the fan are even with 2 adjacent sides of the square. Pin or baste the fan to the square. Then appliqué the fan to the square, turning under 3/16" to 1/4" of the raw edge. Cindy appliquéd by machine, using decorative stitches. Appliqué all 30 squares.

- If you wish, trim away the white background fabric from under the appliquéd fans, clipping carefully 1/4" inside your line of appliqué stitches. Make sure you don't cut the fans! Press the blocks from the back.

ASSEMBLY

- Lay out the completed blocks in 6 horizontal rows of 5. Arrange the blocks as shown in the photo, or position them any way you like.
- Stitch the blocks into rows, then sew the rows together.
- Take 4 of the 1 1/2" x 44" green print strips and join them in pairs, end to end. Stitch these pairs to the left and right sides of the quilt. Press, then trim the ends of the strips even with the edges of the quilt.
- Join the remaining three 1 1/2" x 44" green print strips, end to end. Then cut this long strip in half and sew the 2 resulting strips to the top and bottom edges of the quilt. Press, and trim the ends of the strips as needed.
- Join the 1 1/2" x 44" plaid strips in pairs, end to end, making 4 long strips. Sew one to the left side and one to the right side of the quilt. Press, then trim the ends of the strips. Sew the other 2 strips to the top and bottom edges of the quilt. Press and trim.
- Use the 1" x 44" red print strips in the same way to make the third border.
- Add the outermost border, using the 6" x 44" Christmas print strips in the same way.
- Finish the quilt as described in the *General Directions*. Cindy created a quilting design of holly leaves from the Christmas print in the border and quilted it around the fans. Use the 2 1/2" x 44" strips for the binding. ❦

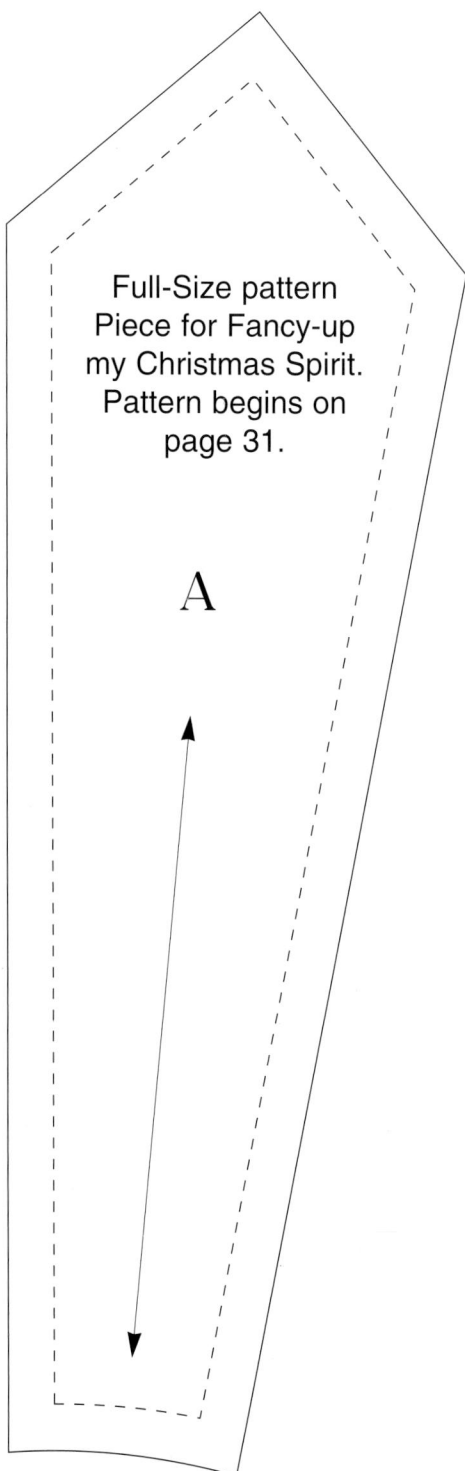

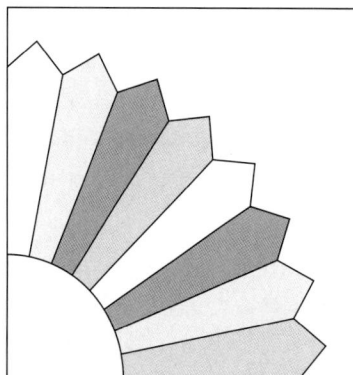

Full-Size pattern Piece for Fancy-up my Christmas Spirit. Pattern begins on page 31.

A